UNDE
HYGGE

The Scandinavian Art of Well-Being
& 32 Craft Ideas
To Get You Comfy and Cozy

Tobias Jan Pedersen

Copyright ©2022 Tobias Jan Pedersen

All Rights Reserved

Table of Contents

Introduction 7
Chapter One: Hygge Explained 8
    Hygge Pronounced "Hoog-Ga" 8
    Understanding Hygge Better 8
Chapter Two: The Five Elements and Three Principals of Hygge .. 10
    The Five Elements of Hygge: 10
    The Three Main Principles of Hygge: 12
Chapter Three: How to Hygge 13
    Hygging Better 13
Chapter Four: The Dimensions of Wellness in Hygge Perspective .. 16
    Mental Health & The Mental Benefits of Hygge 16
    Spiritual Health 17
    Emotional Health 18
    Vocational Health 18
    Social Wellness & The Social Benefits of Hygge 19
    Financial Wellness 22
    What Health and Wellness Has To Do With Hygge? 23
    The Physical Benefits of Hygge 24
Chapter Five: How to Hygge in Winter 25
    Why Are Winters The Most Hygge Time of Year? 25
    Ten Simple Ideas to Hygge in Winter 25
Chapter Six: What is Hygge Interior Design? 33
    How Do I Add A More Hyggelig (Hygge-Like) Style to My Home? 33
    Seven Ways to Add a More Hyggelig Style to Your Home ... 34
Chapter Seven: The Art of Feng Shui and Wabi-Sabi and Their Relationship with Hygge 37
    What Is Feng Shui and How Is It Hygge? 37

What Does Feng Shui Have to Do with Hygge? 38

What Is Wabi-Sabi and How Does It Coincide with Hygge? 39

What Does Wabi-Sabi Have to Do with Hygge? 39

Chapter Eight: Scandinavian Soul Food/Pastimes and Five Ways to Bring Hygge to Your Plate 41

What Is Scandinavian Soul Food, and Where Did The Term Originate From? 41

Five Ways to Bring Hygge to Your Home Plate 42

Three Ingredient Mac and Cheese Recipe 43

What Is "Fika?" 45

Where Did Fika Come From? 46

Enjoy a bit of Fikka at Home with These Two Drinks 46

Chapter Nine: 32 Craft Ideas 48

What Does Crafting and Making Arts Have to Do with Hygge? 48

32 Craft Ideas That Can Help You Feel Comfy & Cozy 48

Knitting 49

Knitting a Beanie 49

Knitting a Blanket (The Arctic Throw Pattern) 51

Knitting a Scarf 51

Knitting a Pair of Slippers 52

Sewing 53

Sewing a Pair of Gloves from Fabric 53

Sewing a Pair of Socks from Fabric 54

Sewing a Pillowcase 55

Sewing a Picnic Blanket 56

Tapestry 58

Moon Phase Wall Art 58

Beach Blanket Tapestry 60

Bedspread Tapestry 60

Photo Backdrop 61
Weaving **63**
   Woven Necklace 63
   Place Mats 65
   DIY Woven Bag 66
   Woven Tea Towel (Warp, Plain Weave) 67
Woodworking **68**
   Making a Bench 68
   Making an Easel 69
   Making a Mini Pallet Coaster 70
   Making a Faucet Coat Hanger 71
Art Therapy **73**
   Flower Art 73
   Portrait Painting 74
   Finger Painting 74
   Drawing/Doodling 75
Pottery **76**
   Vase with Handles 77
   Clay Plate (Slab Technique) 78
   Clay Mug 78
   Clay Planter 79
Mind and Body **81**
   Candle Making 81
   Tools and Safety Equipment 81
   How to Make a Basic Container Candle? 91
   Soap Making 93
   Safety Gear and Equipment Needed 94
   The Rebatching Method for Soap Making 98
   Simple Soap Recipe for Pure Glycerin 100

Four Natural Colourants 102
Clay Face Mask 105
Sensual Massage Oil 106
Chapter 10: Incorporating Hygge on a Budget 107
Hygging on a Budget 107
Conclusion 109

Introduction

Denmark is typically described as one of the happiest places in the world, and a study shown in the New World Happiness report states that Denmark was ranked among the top three happiest countries out of the 155 countries surveyed. A distinction the country earned for several consecutive years. It would be safe to say that the Hygge lifestyle has been fully integrated into the Danish culture and cultural psyche.

Isn't that why the Danes are so happy? This book will give you a better understanding of what Hygge entails, such as different craft ideas and how this is a part of the Hygge lifestyle as well as, Hygge interior design and much more. So grab a packet of sweets or two, light a candle, and cover up under a warm cozy blanket whilst we dive into the Hygge lifestyle. (Your part-way there)

Chapter One: Hygge Explained

Hygge Pronounced "Hoog-Ga"

The word was derived from the Norwegian term for "well-being." Hygge is used as both a noun and adjective in Denmark. The Danish word Hygge/Hygge-ing (Adjective) is an expression often used when one is at peace with themselves, their spouse, and the environment that they are in. This expression has been used over the past couple of years, particularly in the "Winter months.

Another word from where the term Hygge can come from is Hyggja, which translates to "to think" in Old Norse. Also, Hygge could be derived from the Old Norse word Hugr then later becoming Hug which means the soul, mind, and consciousness. Hygge is similar to the German term gemütlichkeit and the Dutch idea of gezelligheid.

You might have heard of the phrase "Hoo-ga," so what does that exactly mean besides being at peace with oneself?

Simply put, hobbies, spending time with friends and family, healthy eating, and living are all examples of Hygge. The cozy and warm lifestyle that Hygge promotes has been a crucial part of Danish culture since the late 1800s, when the word Hygge first appeared in the written language. The theme of Hygge became so popular in the U.K. that it was even included in the Collins Words of the Year for 2016, second only to Brexit.

In 2017 it was America's turn to go crazy for a Hygge inspired lifestyle and jump on the bandwagon. This didn't stop there; the trend also picked up on social media; Pinterest also predicted it would be one of the biggest decor trends of 2017.

Still, Hygge is a very popular term and the philosophy of coziness, homeliness, and a happy lifestyle is ever present across Europe and America.

Understanding Hygge Better

Another term for Hygge is "an art of creating intimacy" (either with yourself or your friends and home). While there's no clear definition to describe Hygge, there are, however, several words that can be used interchangeably, such as;

- Coziness
- Charm
- Happiness
- Security
- Familiarity
- Comfort
- Reassurance
- Simpleness
- Kinship
- Contentedness

The Danes created Hygge because they wanted to survive boredom, dark, cold, and sameness. This was a way for them to celebrate and break up the mundane or harsh. With many cold dark days, the simple act of enjoying a cup of coffee or lighting a candle can make a big difference to one's spirit.

To better understand Hygge, we have to embrace our surroundings. The rain can pour down, but that doesn't stop you from taking a little time out of your day to relax, and take a deep breath in and breathe out. Many people get confused as to how relaxing Hygge is.

To put it simply, as long as you are cozy and in the surroundings that you find relaxing and or soothing, you're on the right track. Taking in your surroundings doesn't necessarily mean you have to wait for it to rain. You can go to the dog park and pet a couple of dogs or two.

You can also go for walks on the beach, watch the clouds pass over you, and listen to the wind blowing in the trees. These are just some simple ways to take in your surroundings and have a better viewpoint on life. There are many other ways, but it's up to you to find the right one. Some of them you will find further in this book.

Chapter Two: The Five Elements and Three Principals of Hygge

The Five Elements of Hygge:

In this chapter, we will be discussing the five elements of Hygge which include:

- Warmth
- Soft Textures
- Color
- Nature
- Uplifting Messages

Warmth: How Does One Add Warmth to A Home?

Warmth is one of the five elements of Hygge, and adding warmth to a home is a relatively easy task to accomplish, even by oneself. By adding warmth to your home/apartment, you can create a more comforting feel for yourself and others.

You can light candles, add warm color themes, or add a succulent or two to achieve a sense of well-being. When it comes to Hygge, warmth is a must, no exception; however, when it comes to adding warmth into your home/apartment, it's your own choice as to what warm elements you might use.

Soft Textures: How Do I Incorporate Them?

Soft textures refer to anything with a dull appearance or a smooth surface with curves instead of rather sharp or distinct edges. By embracing imperfections like a vintage handcrafted piece that shows signs of the maker, this can relax space and, in turn, add to the texture of the room.

This adds a touchable quality in keeping with the Japanese style of wabi-sabi. It's important to factor in raw, natural materials that generally add more depth to a space that can enhance the overall aesthetics of the area. Adding curtains to a living area can soften a room if done correctly, and a quick DIY can make a big difference.

Soft texture colors tend to absorb more light and give off a warmer feel. This is precisely what you'd be looking for if you're interested in Hygge interior design or just to add a cozier feel to your home/apartment.

Color: Why Is Color an Element of Hygge?

Color is an element of Hygge since color, depending on what you use, can add warmth or depth to your home/apartment. It's essential to remember that everyone's opinions differ from which colors seem warm to them, so stay open -minded. There are many different colors to choose from, and the possibilities are almost endless.

However, don't get side-tracked and end up regretting the colors you've chosen. That's why it's always essential to research the colors you want to go for beforehand. Rustic colors are as good a place to start as any.

Nature: Is This Really an Element of Hygge?

Yes, simply put, nature is an element of Hygge. Embracing nature or adding a few plants to your living space can significantly enhance your overall well-being and add a cozy feel to a room. The simple task of going for a walk or collecting some flowers to add to your centerpiece is a great way to get in touch with nature and relax a little.

The Danish concept of Hygge is often seen as a far-away dream for most with today's current pace of life. However, it's crucial to relax, too, as this can significantly impact how you feel and your overall health. It's not always about going outside to embrace nature. You can also enjoy nature from your own home just by cracking open a window and letting the breeze bellow in.

Uplifting Messages and Acts of Kindness: Is This an Element of Hygge?

Some people tend to get confused as to how an uplifting message is an element of Hygge. Simply put, sending a loved one a message that speaks from the heart can make you feel better and uplift their spirits, which in turn is a sense of well-being, which is precisely what Hygge is.

It doesn't necessarily have to be a loved one; it could be a spouse or dear friend; the choice is entirely up to you. It's always good to keep in contact with friends and family, and what better way is there than sending them a message now and then. By doing this, you ensure that you love and miss them as well, as you're doing just fine.

Sometimes that little letter or message you send to someone can really lighten up their day, and there's nothing wrong with that.

The Three Main Principles of Hygge:

Three different words can sum up the three main principles of Hygge. These words include:

- Presence: Being present and mindful as to the environment you are in.
- Pleasure: finding pleasure in life's simple joys and incorporating fun into your life.
- Participation: Being more engaged with the community or other and interpersonal.

Therefore, scientifically speaking, we are the catalysts for our own happiness. Thereby incorporating these three Main Principles of Hygge into our daily lives, we will have more satisfaction, control, and freedom to manage our lives the way we want and need.

Chapter Three: How to Hygge

Hygge can be done relatively quickly. You can be flying solo or with friends, family, and or a loved one; the choice is yours. Simply lighting a candle and embracing the glow that it gives off is considered Hygge. Why do people Hygge? So that they can escape the long, dark, cold, and dull winters. Take a bath and relax with a few candles. This is an excellent way you can Hygge at home.

The concept for the Danish/Scandinavian term Hygge is best described as a feeling of being satisfied or spending time with friends and family. Hygge can be enjoyed with friends or family but tends to be better spent when you're not flying solo. Going for walks on the beach or just sitting down in your favorite spot all count as a way of Hygge; why? That's because you are enjoying the moment that you might be in, whether it be with friends, family, or a loved one.

Hygging Better

There are many forms and ways to Hygge, so let's discuss a couple of ways in which you can enjoy your Hygge lifestyle to the fullest. Here are just a couple of ways to Hygge a little better.

Lighting Candles

Lighting candles is a great way to relax. Not only does the light leave you feeling warm and cozy, but it can also leave your house smelling fragrant and lovely if you opt for scented candles.

Burning Incense

Burning incense-like Sandalwood, cinnamon, and Patchouli; have their own unique smells and fragrances. These smells can leave you feeling relaxed and at peace with yourself.

Having a Glass of Wine with Friends

Drinking a glass of wine with friends," it doesn't need to be fancy," can also help you relax. However, it is best to keep it all in moderation, though.

Using Aromatherapy

Aromatherapy is like using incense; the smells leave the atmosphere pleasant and relaxing.

Playing Relaxing Music

Listening to music that you enjoy is another way to understand Hygge better. The simple task of plugging in some earbuds can, in some cases decrease cortisol,(the stress hormone in the brain), elevate mood, and increase serotonin and endorphin levels (the happy chemicals).

Going for Walks/Strolls

Going for a daily jog or walking your pet is a great way to get in touch with your inner self. Doing so leaves your body fit and healthy. This also increases your overall stamina.

Turning off Unnecessary Electrical Devices

No one wants a T.V. on in the background. Turning off your mobile device dramatically increases the Hygge feel. This allows you to focus on the materialistic things in life, just like the Danes.

Creating Homemade Crafts

Making DIY crafts is a great way to feel Hygge. Try creating paintings or art pieces that give off a warm and cozy feeling.

Adding Rugs to Soften up Some Areas

Placing a rug or soft carpet hide can give a more Hygge feel to your home/apartment.

Reading a Novel or Book

Reading helps you relax but also takes your mind off unwanted stress. This allows you to drift off into a new world and puts your mind at ease.

Partake in Stress-free Cooking Classes

Eating healthy food or food you like, in general, helps you better understand the Hygge experience/feeling. Joining a cooking class can also help you relax because cooking can activate memories like that smell that reminds you of your "grandmother's" house.

Engage in Friendly Conversations with Friends and Family.

Just having a friendly chat with a loved one or having a laugh is a great way to keep up with friends and family. This leaves you feeling a sense of "appreciation" and "gratification.

Scattering Rose Petals: That's Very Hygge

Being romantic with a spouse is an excellent way of showing affection. Scattering rose petals and lighting some candles to set the mood is very Hygge.

Try an Adult Coloring Book

This might sound childish, but this is a great way to relax. Nothing has to be perfect. Just let you mind-run wild and let your stencil do the talking. Use warm and relaxing colors to add a little more Hygge to your home.

Reflect on Your Days with Gratitude

It's hard sometimes to embrace the little things, so why not take a step back and reflect on your day with a bit of gratitude. You don't need to go out of your way and do something extraordinary.

Giving Your Animals Toys to Play With

Watching your pets play around or interacting with them is a great way to relieve stress and fatigue.

Chapter Four: The Dimensions of Wellness in Hygge Perspective

- Mental Health
- Spiritual Health
- Emotional Health
- Vocational Health
- Social Wellness
- Financial Wellness

Mental Health & The Mental Benefits of Hygge

Mental health and Hygge go hand in hand because, like stated, mental health is the state of well-being. When it comes to Hygge and the mental benefits, the list is endless, from lowered stress levels to an improvement in anxiety and depression symptoms, etc. Not only will this lead to an overall improvement in your mental health this also improves your health in general.

However, this doesn't necessarily mean that because you suffer from slight depression or anxiety that you can't experience Hygge. Simply put, it's just as essential to keep your mental health in mind when trying to achieve a sense of well-being.

Some Mental Health Benefits Include:

- A clearer mind
- Increased feeling of optimism
- Promotes anti-anxiety
- Increases your productivity

Five Ideas for Improving Your Mental Health (Which are Very Hygge)

Reading a Book or Novel

Reading helps you to relax and takes your mind off unwanted stress. This allows you to drift off into a new world and puts your mind at ease.

Exercise

Exercising is a great way to keep healthy. Not only will this relieve some stress from a long day, but it also increases the heart rate, which then pumps more oxygen to the brain. This aids the release of happy hormones (Endorphins) to the brain.

Mindfulness

Staying mindful is a great way to improve your mental health. Staying mindful allows you to focus on the present and accept it without judgment.

Give to Others

Giving a gift to a friend or sending a letter to a loved one can give you a sense of purpose that helps to create positive feelings.

Maintaining Good Relationships

Keeping in contact with friends and family is always highly recommended. Not only will this increase the bonds you have with your friends and family, but this also leads to a happier way of life.

Spiritual Health

The definition of Spiritual Health has three dimensions; individualistic, religious, and material world-oriented. According to participants, this entails knowledge and practices based on divine unity to have more active relationships with oneself. The term "spirit" was derived from the Latin word "spiritus" (meaning courage, breath, soul, or vigor) and "spirare" (to breathe).

Five Characteristics of Spirituality Include:

- Value
- Transcendence
- Connecting with yourself, family, the environment, God/supreme power.
- Meaning
- Becoming the growth and progress in life:

Hygge coincides with spiritual health simply because if you're unhappy, you're not going to get in touch with that Hygge feeling. Hygge is all about getting in touch with yourself or friends and family; however, you can do this alone, but most often, it's better to spend that time with a friend or loved one.

Emotional Health

Emotional health and Hygge need to coincide; this is simply because you can't live happily if your emotions aren't in check. It's been mentioned previously that individuals who have a better time handling emotional problems tend to deal better with day-to-day issues, whether they are good or bad.

You don't necessarily need to be emotionally stable to practice Hygge. Still, it would be recommended that you address these problems before you try to experience Hygge or live a Hygge lifestyle.

Here Are A Few Tips to Improve Your Emotional Health

1. Express your feelings in an appropriate way
2. Think before you act
3. Be aware of your reactions and emotions
4. Strive for balance
5. Manage stress
6. Connect with others
7. Take care of your health
8. Stay positive
9. Find purpose and meaning

Vocational Health

Hygge and Vocational health are very similar too. Vocational health or vocational wellness is defined as gaining enrichment from one's work and personal satisfaction. It doesn't matter if it is academic work or a job after graduation. Setting goals is a great way to start; however, be realistic when setting them. You don't want to let yourself down. Stick to things you're good at or find something you like doing.

Making sure that your vocational health is in check is a great way to achieve a sense of fulfillment. Not only will this uplift your spirits, but this, in turn, helps you lead a better way of life in general. Hygge coincides with vocational health because if one workplace or space they may occupy is uncomfortable or unpleasant, they might find it hard to interact with others.

Gaining satisfaction from one's work or that feeling you get when you've achieved a satisfactory result for whatever you might be doing. Well, that's Hygge, and don't let anyone tell you differently. To better understand Hygge, you must know what Vocational health is.

Tips for Setting Yourself Reasonable Goals:

- Explore your values, skills, and interests and how they can relate to your career choices.
- Keep your eyes open for major job opportunities that might be available to you or work that's just up your alley.
- Challenge barriers and societal sec roles that limit huge job opportunities
- Work on effective job-related skills such as confrontation, feedback, time management, assertiveness, active listening, motivation, etc.
- Discover the relationship between your primary career choice and other parts of your life.
- Choose a job career that reflects your interests, skills, values, and preferences.
- Keep in mind many people change their major and change career directions many times in life. It's natural.

Small Tip

Keep these minor suggestions in mind when creating your own goals, and I'm sure this will help you. There's no need to rush in and set unrealistic goals; keep that in mind when writing up your goals. Even if you don't know what career choice you might follow, there is no harm in doing a little research beforehand.

Social Wellness & The Social Benefits of Hygge

Social wellness is a term that refers to the relationships we have with our friends, family, and loved ones and how we interact with others. The relationships that we have can offer support through difficult or harsh times. It's crucial to balance your social life with your professional life and academics.

Social wellness also includes balancing the unique need for romantic relationships with other aspects of your life. Maintaining an optimal level of social wellness enables you to build positive relationships with others. Social wellness and Hygge are very similar, if not a perfect match for each other.

Like Hygge, social wellness is all about bonds and the time you spend with family and loved ones. Being with friends and family can significantly increase your overall mood, which can help strengthen the bonds between them. In a Hygge focused lifestyle, there is a large emphasis on forming bonds with friends and loved ones.

Suggestions on How to Enhance Your Social Wellness

1. Make sure to keep in touch with friends and family.
2. Join an organization or club.
3. Reflect on your social needs and yourself.
4. Start practicing self-disclosure.

When we feel emotionally safe and comfortable, we are more likely to nurture connections with others and reach out to friends and family. Hanging with family, friends, and loved ones helps us create a sense of connection and belonging.

Research shows us that this impacts our well-being and health and makes us feel more confident when connecting with others. This allows us to feel safer around others and enables us to take risks that we might not have previously.

Five Ideas to Improve Your Social Health Using Hygge:

1. Spending Time with Friends and Family

This improves your self-confidence and self-worth, increasing your sense of belonging and purpose. In order to have a pleasant time with your friends, relatives, loved ones, or even solo, try Fredagsmus.

Fredagsmys a Scandinavian Game

You're probably wondering what Fredagsmys is? Fredagsmys is a massive deal in Scandinavia-especially in Norway and Sweden. The Danes have their Fredagshygge; this is not as strict as Fredagsmys. Fredagsmys is a household game that you can play with friends and family.

Rules:

1. Fredagsmys must happen on a Friday.
2. Fredagsmys can be played alone but is better when played with friends and family members, so you have someone to share the snacks with. So those elastic waistbands can stay in hiding for just a while longer.
3. Fredagsmys is called Fredagskos, and the Danes call it Fredagshygge; however, they are less strict about the following points, which mainly apply to Norway and Sweden.
4. On Fridays, we eat "Tacos." this might not sound Scandinavian, but it really is.
5. These tacos generally consist of guacamole, diced tomato, cheese, corn, and whatever else you might fancy. The choice is yours to make. I would highly recommend adding feta cheese or plain old cheddar if you want to be boring.
6. Fredagsmys consists of both sweet and savory snacks.
7. Fredagsmys even has its own song just to get you in the right mood, both a Swedish and Norwegian version, but both mean the same thing," No Crisps No Fredagsmys."
8. There have to be crisps on the table, and you can forget the dip that is crucial. Cheese doodles are also a good choice but are primarily found in addition to crisps.
9. Just in case you were wondering, no, Fredagsmys is not the time to go on a diet. Although if you insist, you can always add crudites. This is just another fancy word for sliced crunchy vegetables; these can be dipped too.
10. The sweet stuff It's all about pick and mix. A big bowl is usually used, or a specific bowl bought just for that occasion if possible, it should have the words" sweets" or" candy" on the side. This usually contains everything from salty licorice as well as soft and fluffy marshmallows, speckled with super sour fruity and

chocolate bits. The best part about pick and mix is you can choose your favorite; we won't judge.
11. Chocolate bars are also acceptable in addition to the pick and mix. Some Swedes say you should have at least one bar of Marabou chocolate. In Norway, the equivalent would be a freia. (A Norwegian Chocolate)These big bars can be shared between you or not if you are going solo.
12. Watching tv is essential. Playing board games is a good substitute but makes eating slightly harder. In Norway, they watch" Gullrekka," which is not a program but a collective term for the biggest shows, shown on a Friday night.
13. Done right, Fredagsmys will leave you passed out on the sofa with a face full of tacos, crisps, dips, and sweets without wanting to clear the table before you go to sleep.
14. Eating the leftover crisps is perfectly acceptable for the following Saturday morning, and if you have kids, that just means a little more snooze time.

2. Getting Organized

This enables you to relieve some stress and allows you to feel more open to change.

3. Keeping up with Hobbies/Interests

This is another excellent way to improve your social health. Finding a new hobby or something that might interest you can help you make new friends and also help you interact more with society.

4. Building Skills

When it comes to Hygge building skills is also another great way to improve your social health. Building skills can often lead to new friendships being born and help you to interact more with others. In short, build skills that will help you achieve a sense of well-being and help you lead a happier Hyggelig lifestyle.

Financial Wellness

Financial wellness, otherwise known as" financial well-being," which refers to a person's overall financial health and the absence of money-related stress—well-being that consists of mental, physical, and financial wellness. Being financially stable can make your life a lot easier.

However, this doesn't always bring happiness. Allowing yourself to go on a crazy spending spree may make you feel good at the time; however, this doesn't last long, unlike spending a day with friends and family at the beach where you will have memories for a lifetime.

You might be wondering how Hygge and Financial health coincide? That's a pretty simple question to answer and doesn't take too much explaining. In short, if you're financially stable, it's easier to experience Hygge.

One of the main reasons Hygge coincides with Financial health is that if you're in a good spot financially, you'll have a good overall sense of well-being. This makes it easier to enjoy life and embrace the little things.

What Health and Wellness Has To Do With Hygge?

Having discussed the Dimension of wellness, we more or less know what the dimensions of wellness entail. However, this doesn't necessarily mean you have to have all of the above to achieve a sense of well-being. Focus on one of the six main dimensions and work your way up. You don't need to have all the dimensions of wellness to experience Hygge.

Simply put, by focusing on one of the dimensions of wellness and achieving a sense of well-being, whether it be through your financial health, social fitness, etc. This doesn't necessarily mean that you will need to buy the most expensive car to achieve a sense of well-being; you can be spending time with friends and family, that's a form of social wellness.

And Mental Health plays an essential role in achieving a sense of well-being by pursuing relevant goal setting. Enjoying life and openly participating in community projects or helping your local club by passing out flyers is a great way to interact with people. Not only that, but this, in turn, can help boost your overall mental health, leading to a better way of life.

The Physical Benefits of Hygge

The physical benefits of Hygge are almost endless and when it comes to a Hygge-style environment. Hygge can promote a safe or comforting atmosphere; this enables you to feel more relaxed in the space you occupy and allows you to achieve a sense of well-being through relaxation.

Five Ideas for Improving Your Physical Health with Hygge:

Sleep

Sleep is crucial when it comes to improving your physical health. Not only will this enable you to function better but also enables you to become a more active individual in society.

Limit Technology

No one wants a T.V. on in the background. Turning electronics devices off allows you to focus on the more materialistic things in life, just like the Danes.

Setting your Priorities

When we want to incorporate a Hygge lifestyle, it's crucial to remember that setting your priorities is just as important. If you'd like to achieve a sense of well-being, this is a must.

Get Fresh Air

Going outdoors and enjoying some fresh air is also a great way to improve your physical health. This means you can take a step back and embrace the great outdoors and Mother Nature.

Making Time for Yourself

Spending time with friends is an excellent way to Hygge but don't forget that making time for yourself is essential too. This enables you to concentrate more on the present and improves your overall physical health.

Chapter Five: How to Hygge in Winter

Why Are Winters The Most Hygge Time of Year?

Winter is by far the most Hygge time of year. Why? Because it's the time to knit scarves, blankets, and mittens. It's the time of year that's best enjoyed with friends and family sitting by a bonfire roasting marshmallows. It's possible to Hygge alone, but more than often, Hygge is joining with loved ones in a relaxed atmosphere.

Another reason why winter is the most Hygge time of year for the Scandinavians is because they have very long, dark, and cold winters. At 8:47 am, in January, the sun rises and then sets at 2:55 pm, and in December, the sun rises at 8:41 am and sets at 3:31 pm.

Ten Simple Ideas to Hygge in Winter

Idea One: Throw a Sledding Bash

Taking a moment to simply sit back and just live in the moment is something that has unfortunately been disappearing from our daily lives for people worldwide. Technology has robbed us of moments where you can make connections. As such, there is no better way to correct this than by throwing a sledding bash.

Whereby, having everyone around enjoying the thrill of a sled ride and the warmth of hot chocolate afterward is the best way to get cozy. Alternatively, you could throw whatever type of party you want with whatever theme. The whole point is to be able to make connections without the constant interruptions caused by technology.

It's the simple things in life that we forget to appreciate, and by having those you care about around you experiencing the moment with you, you can create the perfect Hygge atmosphere.

Step One: Ensure that you have snow

Ensure that the amount of snow is at least 2-4 inches or five to ten centimeters.

Step Two: Set the tone

It would be an ideal idea to make a couple of invitations, and why not spice things up a little and make the invitations decorative by cutting them into snowflakes or perhaps a pair of mittens to suit that winter. Alternatively, you can pick any decorative style or pattern that suits your theme or makes you feel a certain way.

Step Three: Get some sweets

The secret here is salty-sweet snacks. You can even opt for ready-made caramel syrup, melted and drizzled over popcorn if you'd like that is.

Step Four: Grab your sled

Time to grab your sled and get some friends and tackle a hill or two.

Step Five: Serve a hot beverage

Take out the hot chocolate and add some marshmallows. Who can say no to that?

Step Six: Set up a garnish station with sweets

Allow guests to be able to customize their drinks with their own toppings of their own choosing. This allows the activity to be more inviting and exciting, especially if children are involved.

Step Seven: Let the food do the talking

Perhaps you might want to decorate the food. There's nothing wrong with that. You must keep in mind the theme you are going for.

Step Eight: Keep everything within easy reach

You can't forget the little ones who want sweets too.

Step Nine: Family Time

After a long day of sledding, sitting down with friends and family is a great way to relax. And partake in some social wellness that the whole party can benefit from

Idea Two: Build a winter bonfire

A winter bonfire is perfect for creating a comfy and cozy atmosphere. That is what Hygge is all about. Most individuals would be left wondering why a winter bonfire is Hygge. Well, think about gathering around a warm fire, with the sounds and smells of the wood flooding your senses, dressed in a warm coat surrounded by those you love most. What could be more Hygge than that?

Step One: Gather firewood

The wood can be slightly wet; however, it burns better when dry.

Step Two: Stack your wood

Whether you're using the teepee method, log cabin, or Swedish flame, it doesn't matter; they are all bonfires. However, the most straightforward method for building a bonfire would be the teepee method.

Step Three: Grab some kindle

This is what will get the fire going. You can use any small twigs/sticks as the kindle, just nothing too big as this can cause difficulty when starting the fire.

Step Four: Light your fire.

Using a lighter or a match, light the kindle gentle blow on the fire once an amber has formed. Grab the marshmallows and enjoy!

Idea Three: Visit a Friend

The cold and dark months of winter encourages most individuals to remain indoors. This fact is especially true when it comes to the Danish; however, alone is typically not what they have in mind. When it comes to the Danish, togetherness and winter, go hand in hand because nothing is better than snuggling up with a blanket and someone you love.

The best part is you are not limited to simply staying indoors; you can always participate in an activity together such as going to the movies or taking a trip to the mall. By visiting a friend, you not only let them know you are thinking of them and that you care, but you are also participating in bettering your social and mental health and wellness all through simply practicing some Hygge.

Step One: Send a message

Send a message to the friend you'd like to visit this way they know beforehand. No one wants unexpected arrivals unless they are surprised.

Step Two: Set a date

Guarantee you check the weather and plan correctly. You do not want to go out when it's pouring with rain, now do you?

Step Three: Go and visit your friend

Why not spend the time at the beach or go to the movies? The choices are nearly endless.

Idea Four: Embrace Seasonal Produce

Cooking in the winter with seasonal produce is not only better for the environment, but it's also more cost-effective and healthy for you. Hygge is all about embracing nature and using fresh seasonal produce wherever possible. By incorporating seasonal ingredients into your winter dishes, you will nourish your mind and your body.

However, you do not have to only focus on embracing seasonal produce only in winter; rather, you can adopt an all-year-round approach to using ingredients that are in season. Thus you are ever closer to adapting that Hyggelig lifestyle.

Step One: Go to the Markets

Make sure you plan properly. Find out from local community members as to when the best time to buy local produce would be in each season.

Step Two: Get what you need, not what you want (Optional)

It's smarter to buy items you need; however, buying a snack here and there is totally acceptable.

Idea Five: Consume a New Hot Beverage

Trying new beverages and moving out of your comfort zone is a great way to start living a cozier lifestyle. That being said, the art of sitting down with a hot cup of something steamy and delicious is always enticing, not to mention oh so Hygge.

Step One: Go to a local restaurant

You might have one already in mind; if not, why not try someplace new.

Step Two: Order a new drink

You don't need to go outside your comfort zone, maybe stick to flavors that you like and branch out from there.

Idea Six: Invite Friends and Family for Brunch

When hosting a get-together, it doesn't necessarily need to be limited to vibrant cocktails and summer decks. Inviting family and friends over for a hearty brunch where they can listen to smooth jazz music (or whatever your interpretation of cozy music is) and enjoy warm and delicious food. At the same time, conversing and socializing to create stronger and more meaningful connections, all with the help of Hygge.

Step One: Send your family and friends a message

Send them a message inviting them over for lunch.

Step Two: Set a date

Plan a date that best suits you so you won't be busy. Keep in mind that others might have plans too, so try to plan accordingly.

Step Three: Plan your meals

Make sure you find out from your friends and family what they might want to eat that evening, as you do not want to serve a dish that your guest might find unappealing.

Step Four: Light a candle or two

Setting the table, why not add some candles? This will relax the mood.

Step Five: Enjoy your meal

Share some jokes with friends and family whilst you enjoy your meal, perhaps tell a story or talk about a past event.

Idea Seven: Take in more vitamin D

One of the root causes of depression, especially seasonal depression, stems from a lack of vitamin D. What is vitamin D? Vitamin D comes from the sun and is essential for regulating your moods and helping to alleviate and lessen the effects of depression.

That being said, when it comes to your mental health, take advantage of the benefits the sun has, and you will be well on your way to achieving that Hygge balance as you will feel more refreshed and ready to take on new challenges.

Step One: Put some shoes on

Grab that pair of dusty sneakers and slip them on, or maybe a pair of shoes that you find comfortable.

Step Two: Grab your water bottle

Don't forget your water bottle; you don't want to get dehydrated.

Step Three: Go outside

Walk around or maybe jog the choice is yours; you're still getting your daily vitamin D.

Idea Eight: Assist Someone by Shovelling their Curb

A simple act of kindness tends to go the extra mile, so why not offer to help someone shovel their snow or assist with something else they may need. How is this Hygge, you may be wondering? When it comes to experiencing Hygge, the feeling of togetherness seems to rise to the front more often than others. So, what better way to experience Hygge than by helping someone else feel that sense of togetherness with you.

Step One: Put some warm clothes on

Putting some warm clothes on ensures that your chances of getting sick are drastically decreased. Not only that, but this prevents hyperthermia from setting in.

Step Two: Grab your shovel and safety boots

It would be an excellent idea to wear a pair of safety boots while working. It's always better to be safe than sorry, don't forget to grab the shovel while you're at it.

Step Three: Go ask the neighbors

There's nothing wrong with helping someone here or there. This not only helps build character but also helps provide us with a sense of gratification.

Idea Nine: Partake in Winter Sports

By partaking in winter sports like sledding and ice skating etc., you are essentially exercising your body as well as partaking in an enjoyable hobby that you find relaxing and exciting.

Hobbies make up a big part of the Hygge lifestyle, and by doing group sports, you can incorporate that same sense of togetherness that is highly beneficial to your health. However, winter sports are not the only sports you can do; just about any old sport will do no matter the season.

Step One: Find a sport that interests you

You might like skating, or perhaps longboarding, so why not look into snowboarding. The concept is relatively the same, just on wheels.

Step Two: Invest in the equipment you need (Optional)

Make sure you have all the correct equipment; however, most centers will have equipment that you can hire out for use.

Step Three: Ask a friend to join you

You might have more fun this way, allowing you to form stronger bonds with them.

Step Four: Enjoy your day out

Share a couple of laughs or consume a warm beverage as long as you're having fun. That's all that matters.

Idea Ten: Learn a Constellation

Learning a constellation is a great way for you to explore and get in touch with nature and your surroundings. Moreover, it can also be a fantastic hobby that involves minimal spending, unless, of course, you want to take it further and buy a telescope; these can typically be quite pricey.

However, nothing says Hyggelig more than outdoor activities, so don't worry about buying because all you have to do is just look up to appreciate what is already there.

Step One: Do some research

Find a constellation that interests you and determine which season is the best time to view it. It's important to remember that the Winter months are generally the best time to stargaze.

Step Two: Choose the correct day

It's important to remember that the best time to view the constellations is when the moon is not at its fullest. This can cause light to block out some stars making it harder to view them.

Step Three: Grab a blanket

You don't want to be sitting down on a hard rock /log, so opt for a blanket and use this to lie down on so you can properly embrace the beauty of the stars.

Step Four: Try not to fall asleep

When stargazing, one can fall asleep, so just be prepared and ensure you have all the correct equipment to tackle the night. If you fell asleep, don't worry, you can always do it again the next time, provided the weather is acceptable.

Chapter Six: What is Hygge Interior Design?

Hygge interior design is the interior design style embodying the Danish concept of Hygge. The simple feeling of feeling content within the home and with life's pleasures. This may vary depending on your personality and culture. It would be in your best interest to research some neutral color themes beforehand, as neutral colors are a crucial part of Hygge interior design.

It's all about bringing a vibrant and comforting atmosphere into your home, thereby creating a stronger sense of intimacy. Hygge-style is not about filling your home up with clutter or buying expensive pieces of artwork. More simply put, it's a feeling of coziness. When Hygge interior design is incorporated into your home, it can bring a sense of well-being or contentment.

How Do I Add A More Hyggelig (Hygge-Like) Style to My Home?

Whether you want to incorporate Hygge design into one room or perhaps all rooms, stocking up on candles is an excellent way to start. How you may wonder? Adding candlelight that gives off a warm, welcoming glow can give off a more Hyggelig feel to your home/apartment, and that's precisely what you want. Also, simply setting up a rug and chair in a dull corner to read one of your favorite authors' books can create a Hegglig feel.

It's not always about purchasing the most expensive house items. Simply put, it is the art of creating intimacy within your home through the use of neutral color tones and items that make your home cozier to live in. These colors and tones will vary depending on your own personal preferences. Below we will delve deeper into what exactly Hygge interior design is.

Seven Ways to Add a More Hyggelig Style to Your Home

Option One: Layer Textures and Materials

When it comes to Hygge interior design, colors such as green, brown, and grey are all considered to be rustic colors. When it comes to choosing a rustic color tone for your home or apartment, it's a good idea to keep those types of colors in mind. These colors are generally used in interior design because they lend a warm cozy feel to the interior.

Make sure you focus on comfort and practicality by adding textural elements around, as this will balance out cleaned-lined furniture and create a more warm and sensory experience. Adding woven rugs and knit tapestries to an area can add coziness and texture to all levels of the space.

Option Two: Embrace Simplicity

When it comes to styling the interior of your home, it's essential to keep it simple and cater to the sweet delights of home. You can achieve this by adding a few books and plants or perhaps a few baskets for small organizations. Not only will this bring in the Scandinavian minimalist aesthetic, but it also promotes relaxation by keeping your space uncluttered.

You can layer in cozy decor too that focuses on comforts such as trays for coffee and tea or vases for plants and flowers. While adding simplicity is the key to this look, sharing moments of joy and delight with friends and family is just as important.

Option Three: Create a sense of Calm

Hygge is all about feeling comfy in order to create a sense of calmness in your household. You should start with a neutral color palette that is high contrast, such as bright whites and lots of natural light.

In order to keep the high-contrast palette from feeling too bold, incorporate off-whites and different colors of brown to help soften the feel of your room or house. It's a good idea to research what color theme you might use because rushing as this can lead to a purchase of unwanted paint color.

Option Four: Create Cosy Corners

Many people love creating smaller moments of coziness within a larger space. It's always a good opportunity to start with a chair placed on a rug with a hand-knitted blanket covering most of the chair. Use a chair that you feel comfortable in and can curl up into if need be. Surround your area with books and candles. This will leave your space feeling more comfortable and relaxing.

Option Five: Centre Yourself with Warmth and Cosiness

By hanging heavy drapery over the windows and placing plenty of candles around wherever you might be sitting is a great way to add warmth and coziness to your home. You can also add some greenery which will add more ambiance. Ultimately, the choice is yours when creating a warm and cozy atmosphere in your home or apartment.

Option Six: Establish Some Ambiance

It's important to remember when it comes to embracing Hygge, candles and fireplaces aren't just for decoration. If you'd like to achieve a great vibe and ambiance, they have to be lit. You can do this relatively quickly by lighting the fireplace or candles to celebrate an event or simply cozying up next to a loved one during the long cold winter months.

Playing some relaxing music or throwing down some rose petals for your loved one is also a great way to add a Hygge ambiance. The word ambiance is just another fancy term for a feeling associated with a person, thing, or place.

So don't be deterred from creating a little ambiance here and there for friends, family, or loved ones. This can lighten your mood and leave you feeling more relaxed after a long day of watching the kids or a hard day at work.

Option Seven: Gather Around the Table with Friends, Family, and Loves Ones

Giving special attention to your dining area is another critical keynote to keep in mind when adding Hygge elements to your dining table. The dining table should have special attention paid to it as doing so can give the area a more Heggelig feel to your home or apartment.

Ensuring your dining-room table is clutter-free and adding a few Hyggelig ornaments like a rustic-looking bowl are two Hyggelig aesthetics of the room. It's imperative to remember not to use too many ornaments, as this can remove the room's Hyggelig aesthetic.

It's not just ornamented either; you can also add greenery to your table. It doesn't always have to be an ornament. The choice is yours, and the list of things to add is almost endless.

Chapter Seven: The Art of Feng Shui and Wabi-Sabi and Their Relationship with Hygge

What Is Feng Shui and How Is It Hygge?

Hygge, Feng Shui, and Wabi Sabi are the three most prominent ancient philosophies and aesthetics. In the same vein, Feng Shui, Wabi-Sabi, and Hygge are all popular design practices that help to achieve a stress-free and homey atmosphere. In this chapter, we will focus on Feng Shui and Wabi-Sabi and how these practices not only give your home, office, or apartment a makeover but also how they offer many psychological benefits.

These benefits aid in maintaining your overall wellness and self-care. With that in mind, it often becomes necessary to incorporate new things in order to change your style to suit your current needs and feelings. This urge to adopt a new healthier lifestyle, get organized, and incorporate more self-care and inspiration into your routine has spread throughout the world like wildfire. As such, how you decide the design of your home, office or apartment has an overall impact on your well-being.

Therefore, whether you're looking for harmony and balance in your office, home, or apartment, the art of Feng Shui has got you covered. Looking deeper, the term Feng Shui translates to "Water" (Shui) and "Wind" (Feng). Feng Shui works on the premise that the world is driven by unseen forces. The idea behind this is to unblock the way so that the forces can flow freely and create balance in your life (or space).

It has been widely dismissed that Feng Shui is an old Chinese myth or fad for kooky new agers. However, Feng Shui's goal is to position the elements in order to optimize Chi. What is Chi? Chi is the positive energy flow that places emphasis on physical and mental health, success, and healthy relationships. Moreover, Feng Shui advocates claim that it can improve everything from wealth and well-being to harmony in the home.

What Does Feng Shui Have to Do with Hygge?

When it comes to Hygge, Feng Shui plays a crucial role in achieving harmony and balance. When we try to incorporate Feng Shui into your Hyggelig style apartment, it's important to keep in mind the five elements of Feng shui.

Earth

Earth is the symbol of balance and stability. Bringing elements such as crystals, stones, and landscape imagery can help you stay stable and grounded. Doing so allows us to create a more harmonious environment which enables us to Hygge better.

Fire

The symbol of energy and passion. Using your fireplace, lighting some candles, or just adding the color red can add the element of fire into your space, representing volatility and transformation. By doing so, you're incorporating Hygge into your lifestyle, which in turn helps to provide a greater sense of well-being.

Wood

The symbol of vitality and growth. Adding simple wooden furniture or a few succulents can promote personal growth, and by doing so, you incorporate Hygge into your life/apartment.

Water

The symbol of serenity and wisdom. Simply adding water elements such as fountains, aquariums, and reflective surfaces like mirrors can help promote relaxation and clarity. This allows us to better incorporate Hygge into our daily lives and, in turn, enables us to achieve a better sense of well-being.

Metal

The symbol of logic and intelligence. By integrating metal into your designs like sculptures, frames, or beams to support knowledge and mental sharpness, this can help you to understand Hygge as a whole better.

Take Note

When talking about Feng Shui and how it coincides with Hygge, it's important not to confuse them with the five elements and three principles of Hygge. It's essential to keep in mind that you do not need all of the five elements of Feng Shui to understand Hygge better, let alone incorporate them. However, it would be ideal to include at least one of the five elements from either Hygge or Feng Shui into your home/apartment to help add to that Hyggelig style of living.

What Is Wabi-Sabi and How Does It Coincide with Hygge?

Described as "beauty in imperfection," Wabi-Sabi originated in China with its history rooted in Zen Buddhism, which later evolved into a Japanese movement linked to the country's famous tea ceremonies.

The term Wabi-Sabi cannot be easily translated due to the fact that the practice is so rich in history, and the meaning of the word has changed over the centuries. "Wabi" is defined as "rustic simplicity" or "understanding elegance" with a focus on a less-is-more mentality.

"Sabi" typically refers to "taking pleasure in the imperfect." Flawed beauty is fully embraced in the Wabi-Sabi philosophy as ancient Japanese royalty saw that embracing imperfection is one of the key steps in achieving enlightenment.

What Does Wabi-Sabi Have to Do with Hygge?

Hygge and Wabi-Sabi are design and lifestyle movements from two very different cultures that, at first glance, might appear different. Still, upon closer inspection, they actually contain a lot of similarities. However, the emphasis on coziness is perhaps the biggest differentiator between Hygge and Wabi-Sabi.

Wabi-Sabi tends to focus more on imperfections than Hygge does, and at the same time, Hygge tends to focus more on coziness than Wabi-Sabi does. However, their underlying principles are very similar, and they both rely on the idea of authenticity, simplicity, and craftsmanship.

Both Wabi-Sabi and Hygge find the passage of time beautiful, and they don't work to combat it. Hygge and Wabi-Sabi both have an innate connection to nature, authenticity, and rusticity, which translates itself into a connection with natural objects you surround yourself with. Specifically speaking, the philosophy of Wabi-Sabi is to utilize and appreciate natural objects and materials that can withstand the test of time almost identical to that of Hygge.

Chapter Eight: Scandinavian Soul Food/Pastimes and Five Ways to Bring Hygge to Your Plate

In this chapter, we will be discussing what Scandinavian soul food is, where the term "Soul-food" originates from, five ways to bring Hygge to your plate, as well as some simple recipes that one can make at home.

What Is Scandinavian Soul Food, and Where Did The Term Originate From?

Scandinavian soul food is food that, when eating, leaves you feeling warm inside like a hot chicken soup. Scandinavian soul food encompasses a variety of flavor profiles that, when combined, create a hearty and satisfying meal. Most dishes are generally hot, but there are sweet treats too, like pumpkin pie.

Soul food originated in the mid-1960s when people used "soul" to describe African-American culture. At its core, soul food refers to cooking methods passed down through the generations, with its roots in rural areas. When cooking soul food dishes, the go-to ingredients include cornmeal, beans, greens, and pork. The number of soul food dishes pork can be used for is almost limitless.

Not only can pork be used to season vegetables, but it can also be used in pickling staples like pork rinds, pigs' feet, and ears. Soul food should come from the heart and should be made with passion. Food often tells a story and can sometimes bring back a distant memory of the past. It might be a smell that almost takes you back to the time you spent with your mom helping her cook up a Sunday meal.

Understanding the history behind these dishes can help you appreciate them just that little bit more. Soul food is such an essential part of Hygge because cooking can bring your friends and family closer through the bonds of food and, depending on the meal cooked, can create a pleasant atmosphere.

A Few Scandinavian Soul Food Dishes:

- Rye bread
- Meat Balls
- Beef, Pork, Chicken, Eggs And Sea-Food Dishes
- Potato Cakes/Boiled Potatoes (Often Served As A Side Dish)
- Herring (A Type Of Scandinavian Fish)
- Sill (Pickled Herring)
- Falukorv (Falu Sausage)

Five Ways to Bring Hygge to Your Home Plate

Indulge in Some Dessert

Nothing wrong with having a sweet tooth, so why not grab that packet of sweets, crack it open, and share it with friends and family or by yourself if you're not one to share. It doesn't necessarily have to be sweets; you can have savory items too; the choice is entirely up to you.

Pretty up Your Plate

Present the food nicely on a white plate, with the option of garnishing your dish with fresh herbs like spring onion. Nice cutlery can be used, too, just to add to that "pretty" feeling. Some cutlery that can be used is timber knives which adds to the rusticity of a room if that is the theme that you've been aiming for.

Soothe with spices

In Sweden, Christmas is one of the biggest highlights of the winter month. Cloves, Cinnamon, Cardamom, Orange, and Ginger, are all spices that can be used during the winter months as these spices can add to the warm feeling that food can bring and are often regarded as "Feel good ingredients."

Go wild

There's nothing wrong with traveling out of your comfort zone and indulging in a new taste, so why not cook with Swiss chard, Wild asparagus, or artichokes. These vegetables may seem out there, but I can assure you that they are super delicious if cooked correctly.

Savor every mouthful

Take your mind off unwanted stress simply by turning off the phone while you eat since using your device while eating can cause stress. So instead, why not focus on mindful eating? To do this, simply slow down and engage with the eating process, look at how the food smells, tastes, and looks. By doing so, you will begin to enjoy and experience the food more. Below is a simple Scandinavian Mac and Cheese recipe.

Three Ingredient Mac and Cheese Recipe

Ingredients:

- Five Cups Of Milk (1¼L/41.67oz)
- One lb Elbow Macaroni, Dry (455g/16.05oz)
- Two Cups Of Cheese (200g/7.055oz)

Note: *Serves Four*

Small Tip: *Ensure all cooking apparatus is ready beforehand*

Cooking Equipment

- One Large Pot
- One Small Pot
- Grater
- Wooden Spoon For Mixing
- Baking Tray
- Measuring Cup

Cooking Instructions

Step One: Gather Equipment

In a large pot, start boiling the milk on low heat, frequently stirring to prevent the milk from burning or boiling over.

Step Two: Preheat the Stove

Once your milk has reached a rolling boil, add the macaroni and reduce the temperature to a simmer, you can opt to add spices at this point, like salt or paprika.

Step Three: Check the Macaroni

If the macaroni is done, you can check this with a fork. You can begin adding your cheese to your pasta, allowing the cheese to fully melt and mix in with the macaroni.

Step Four: Let the Macaroni Simmer

Leave the macaroni and cheese to simmer for at least 5-10 minutes; this ensures that the cheese melts properly. You must not forget to stir regularly and turn the heat down to medium, as you wouldn't want your glorious mac and cheese to burn now would you?

Step Five: Preheat the Oven

Preheat your oven to exactly 180 degrees Celsius/356 degrees Fahrenheit.

Step Six: Set Aside To Rest

Once the cheese has melted and the pasta is cooked to perfection, you can set the mac and cheese aside to rest whilst you move on to step seven.

Step Seven: Coating the Tray

Coat the inside of the baking tray with wax paper or spray and cook it would be in your best interest to use wax paper as this tends to stick less than other potential coatings.

Step Eight: Take Out the Macaroni

Scoop your mac and cheese out of the pot. Place the mac and cheese inside the baking tray, sprinkling a little cheese on top to add a crispy texture to the outside.

Step Nine: Bake in The Oven

Bake the macaroni and cheese for approximately 15-20 minutes at 180 degrees Celsius/356 degrees Fahrenheit or until the cheese is fully golden brown on top.

Step Ten: Let It Cool Off

After the mac and cheese has reached a golden brown color on top, you can remove it from the oven to cool down or to be served hot.

Small Reminder

It's important to remember that mac and cheese is often served as a side dish but is still considered a soul food dish. This macaroni dish is by far one of the more simple recipes out there for soul food. Mac and cheese is a dish that's often found at family restaurants as you can't really go wrong when it comes to mac and cheese and family time.

What Is "Fika?"

Fika roughly translates to the afternoon "coffee and cake break," and like Hygge, it is more of a feeling and connection than action. Although the two traditions at the forefront are Hygge and Fikka, they both follow the same concept of slowing down.

Fika is such a big part of Scandinavian culture that some companies include clauses in the employee contract allowing Fika breaks. Moreover, in Sweden, it's not uncommon to see them drinking warm beverages in minus ten centigrade (about 14 degrees Fahrenheit.)

Hygge and Fikka offer many ways to build connections and strengthen your bonds with others. Fikka provides us with an excuse to slow down these days; everyone is on a work overload. Fikka, often regarded as "Kos" in Norway, is a concept in which one can take a break from the daily grind. Sitting down and connecting with someone and perhaps having a cup of coffee with a sweet treat is pretty much what fikka is all about.

However, timing is everything, and whether you practice Fikka alone or with friends, the intention is to make time to decompress. With this knowledge in mind, it is crucial to understand that you can practice Fika practically anywhere. Whether you are simply out in the woods or in a nearby park, Fikka is a popular pastime, especially on a sunny day.

Where Did Fika Come From?

As we begin to better understand the meaning behind Fikka (fee-kah), we begin to wonder, where did this saying first surface? The word itself is believed to be the reversal of the syllables in the old term Kaffi, meaning coffee.

Initially, coffee itself was introduced to Sweden in the 18th century; it was considered the proper Fika. However, over the years, the accompanying baked goods, often called fikabröd(Fika bread) -became just as important.

The arrival of pastries in Sweden in the 19th century paved the way for a coffee-and-cake custom enjoyed with friends and family. That's why it's often seen that individuals who practice Fikka are often caught with a sweet in their hands.

It's important to remember that Fikka is regarded by most as more of a pastime than anything else. Some individuals may see Fikka as more of a break for themselves than anything else, which in itself is "Fikka."

Enjoy a bit of Fikka at Home with These Two Drinks

Mumma

This is a traditional Christmas beverage made up of a concoction of other beverages like porter, pilsner, wine, and something sweet and is typically spiced with cardamom. In order to create this traditional spicy beverage, you will need;

- 500ml\16.9oz of Larger
- 500ml/16.9oz of Stout
- 250ml/8.5oz of Lemonade
- 75ml/2.5oz of Madeira
- A splash of gin (Optional)

Process

Pour each liquid into a jug and combine well. Once mixed, transfer into your choice of drinking glasses and enjoy.

Glogg

This is a unique form of mulled wine that is served warm or hot and is typically alcoholic. Glogg is a traditional Nordic drink consumed primarily in winter and especially during Christmas. In order to create this traditional Nordic drink, you will need;

- One bottle of your choice of red wine
- One orange
- Ten Cardamom pods
- Five cloves
- One cinnamon stick
- 200g/7.05oz of castor sugar
- Three slices of peeled fresh ginger
- 50g/1.8oz of sultanas or raisins
- 50g/1.8oz of flaked almonds
- 150ml/5.07oz of Aquavit or Vodka

Process

First, peel away the orange zest into strips, making sure to cut away any pith. Secondly, place the zest into a saucepan with the wine, sugar, cloves, ginger, cardamom, cinnamon, almonds, and sultanas or raisins. Next, Warm the mixture gently for ten to fifteen minutes, ensuring it never reaches a boil. Lastly, mix in the Vodka or Aquavit before serving warm.

Chapter Nine: 32 Craft Ideas

What Does Crafting and Making Arts Have to Do with Hygge?

Many people enjoy the idea of going home and painting a picture or making a simple DIY item. The idea of going home and relaxing while doing something you want can help you feel less stressed after a hard day at work or a hard day of studies.

Being able to go home and do something you enjoy, whether it be painting or crafting or something else entirely, is Hygge. You're currently feeling it provided your feeling a sense of satisfaction or well-being. This doesn't mean you need to purchase the most expensive paints or crafting materials.

Going outside and finding locally sourced materials is an excellent way to ensure that you stay within your budget if you have a budget to begin with. Finding a stick in the wood and sanding it down to add some nails is a perfect idea for a low-cost coat hanger. This is a great way to get in touch with the great outdoors.

32 Craft Ideas That Can Help You Feel Comfy & Cozy

Knitting

Knitting is a fantastic hobby for those who enjoy working with their hands. It truly benefits the mind, the soul, and the body. Taking a closer look at knitting, you will find it not only keeps your mind focused but also improves your strength and dexterity in your hands.

This means that your hand-eye coordination will benefit from such an activity. Moreover, when looking at knitting, it is known to be quite calming and relaxing, all the while keeping you busy for hours alone or with company.

Knitting a Beanie

Supplies:

- Knitting needle size 5 or 8 mm
- Gauge
- Soft wool (1 ball 9440 Light Grey Heather)
- Scissors

Abbreviations:

- k: Knit
- k2tog: Knit 2 sts together
- Cm: centimetres
- Mm: millimeters
- p: purl
- st(s): stitch/es
- Tog: Together
- *or**: This means repeat whatever follows the * or ** as indicated

Pattern Option One: Broken Rib (Over an Even Number of sts)

Row One: (Right side) *k1, p1; repeat from * to the end of the row.

Row Two: purl

Repeat Rows one and two for Broken Rib Pattern

Pattern Option Two: Rib 1x1 (Over an even number of sts)

Row One: (Right side) *k1, p1; repeat from* to the end of the row.

Row Two: Knit the knit sts and purl the purl sts as they appear to end the row. Repeat row two for 1x1 Rib.

Beanie Making Process:

1. Start by casting 86 sts
2. Lower Ribbing (Work in 1x1 Rib until the piece measures about one inch/2-5 cm long from the start; End with a wrong side row).
3. Body (Work in Broken Rib until the pieces measure about 8 inches/20.5 cm from the start; end with a wrong side row).
4. Shape Crown (decrease row (Right side): *k1, p1, k1, ktog, p1, k1, p1, ktog, ptog; repeat from * to last two sts, k2tog-61 sts).
5. Row Two (Purl)
6. Decrease Row Three (*k1. P1, k2tog, p2tog; repeat from * to the last st, k1-41sts.
7. Row Four (Purl)

8. Decrease Row Five (*k2tog, p2tog; repeat from * to last st, k1- 21sts).
9. Row Six and Seven (Repeat rows Four and Five-Eleve sts. Cut the yarn leaving a long tail. Thread the tail through the remainder of the stitches and remove the thread from the needle. Pull together and close the top opening. Sew the side edges together for a back seam).
10. Weave in the ends (Finish)

Knitting a Blanket (The Arctic Throw Pattern)

Supplies:

- Yarn
- Scissors
- Measuring tape
- Tapestry needle
- Knitting needles (9.00 mm circulars that are 36 inches/ 91 cm or longer)

Abbreviations:

- Co: cast off
- Bo: bind off

Blanket Making Process:

1. Row One: *k1, p1; repeat from * to end the end of the row. (74-106 sts)
2. Row Two: p1, k1; repeat from * to the end of the row. (74-106 sts)
3. Repeat Rows One and two until (172-216) are completed or until it has reached your desired length.
4. Bind off/ bo: Cut the yarn, fasten off, and weave in all the ends. (Finish)

Knitting a Scarf

Supplies:

- Knitting gauge tool

- Tapestry needle
- Sharp scissors
- Tape measure
- Crochet hook (For Fringe)
- Stitch markers (Optional)

Scarf Making Process:

1. Cast on 25 stitches with size 8 (U.S)-6 mm knitting needle
2. Row One: *knit
3. Repeat row one until you have created the desired length. (Finish)

Knitting a Pair of Slippers

Supplies:

- U.S. size 7 Knitting needles
- Two ozs 4 inch/ 10 cm weight yarn (Worsted weight)
- Large eye blunt needle
- Sharp scissors

Slipper Making Process:

1. Cast on: (32 Stitches)
2. Begin the pattern: Rows 1-4 knit.
3. Rows Five (Short): Knit 20, turn.
4. Rows Six: Slip row one purlwise, Purl 19 (Repeat rows One through Six seven more times. This will give you a total of Eight short row stripes).
5. Work through: Rows One to Four one more time.
6. Bind off: Leaving a long tail for when cutting the yarn.
7. Sew slippers: (Together)
8. Fold Slippers: Fold the slippers in half, with a separate piece of yarn, sew the back edges together to create the heel.
9. Use a pom-pom: Create a pom pom and sew it to the top of the slipper. (Optional). (Finish)

Sewing

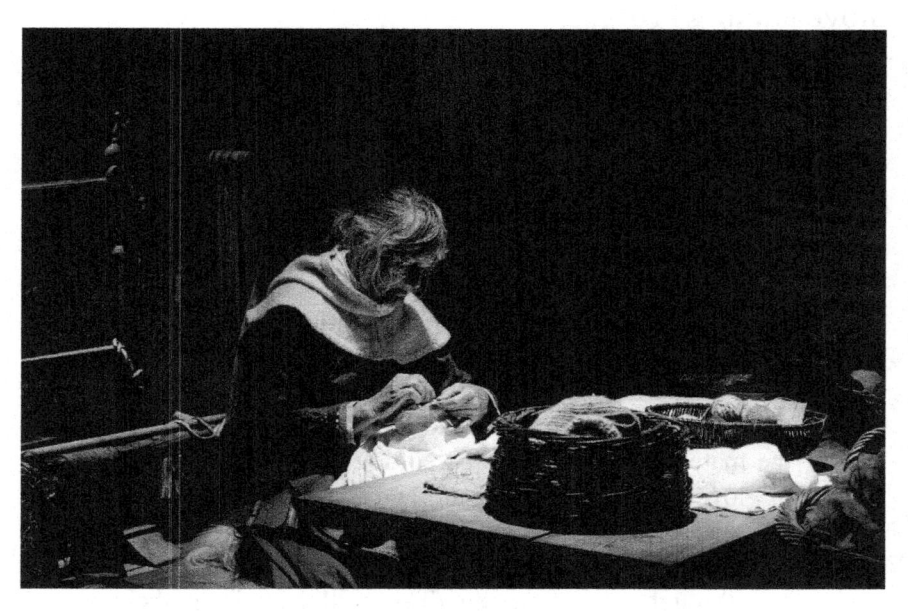

Everyone experiences feelings of stress at least once in their lifetime, and if you've ever found yourself overly frustrated, why not give sewing a try. Among the many benefits of sewing, the primary ones include; improved hand-eye coordination and self-discipline, skill in the fingers, and a healthier mind.

These, however, are not the only benefits; sewing also encourages upcycling of clothes (benefiting the environment by limiting textile waste), promotes creative thinking, and brings communities together.

Sewing a Pair of Gloves from Fabric

Supplies:

- Pen/pencil
- Sewing machine
- Paper
- Scissors
- Fabric (of your choosing) and (must be bigger than your hand)
- 5-10 pins (Depending on the size of your hand)

- Sewing machine

Glove Making Process:

1. Trace your hand: Trace the outline of your hand onto a piece of paper. Be sure to extend the sleeve of the glove to the desired length.
2. Cut your traced hand out: Cut along the line you have outlined on the paper with a pair of scissors.
3. Place the hand on a piece of fabric: Make sure you fold your piece of cloth in two, then place your traced hand onto the fabric.
4. Retrace your hand: Once the hand is in place, place pins into it. Doing so will allow you to be more precise when tracing.
5. Cut the fabric: Once you have finished tracing your hand onto the fabric, begin to cut the fabric, keeping in mind not to move the material too much whilst cutting as this can lead to the pair of gloves being slightly bigger than anticipated.
6. Remove the pins: Remove the pins from the paper and insert pins every 2 to 3 (5.1-7.6 cm) along the ends of the fabric and one through each fingertip (This will help keep the material together while you sew).
7. Sew a straight stitch: Sew the stitch along the outline of the glove. This is where you have traced except for at the glove's opening.
8. Cut the fabric: Cut the excess fabric off; be careful not to cut a hole through any of the stitches as this will create a hole in the glove.
9. Hem: Hem the glove's opening and cut the excess of the thread when you get back to the hem.
10. Turn the glove: Make sure you turn the glove inside out and try it on to make sure it fits.
11. Other hand: To do the other hand repeat the process and follow the same steps (Finish)

Sewing a Pair of Socks from Fabric

Supplies:

- Fabric (should be slightly elastic)
- A sock

- Scissors
- Pins
- Sewing machine
- Pen/marker
- Sewing machine

Sock Making Process:

1. Buy some fabric: you can go and find some fabric at your local DIY store or use some old clothes to repurpose them into a pair of socks (Make sure the material that you are using is slightly elastic).
2. Place your sock onto the fabric: Once the sock has been pinned the sock there, trace around the sock with the pen or marker, ensuring that the color you use is dark enough or has a vibrant enough color to see.
3. Cut the fabric: Cut around the sock, trying to ensure that you cut as close as you can to the cut-out sock to ensure a correct fit.
4. Repeat this process: Follow the same steps to create two cut-outs in total.
5. Place your cut-out socks on top of each other: There shouldn't be a need to worry about which way the fabric faces as it should look the same way on both sides.
6. Pin the socks: Pin the socks together, ensuring that the sock is stacked perfectly before doing so.
7. Sew: Sew around the edge of the sock with a zig-zag stitch pattern, making sure that you do not sew the top hole.
8. Sew a straight stitch: This helps prevent the seam from coming undone.
9. Turn the socks inside out: Pull the sock inside out by reaching into the sock and grabbing the toe. This hides the seam and reveals the other side of the fabric. (Finish)

Sewing a Pillowcase

Supplies:

- Spare pillowcase
- Scissors
- Ruler for measuring

- Fabric
- Pins
- Paper
- Pen/marker
- Sewing Machine

Pillowcase Making Process:

1. Using the spare pillowcase: measure the width and length of the pillowcase in order to get your design lengths.
2. Cut the fabric: Once the pillow has been measured, use the piece of paper as a template and outline the pillow's length using your marker/pen.
3. Repeat the process: Follow the same steps with the other piece of fabric.
4. Sew: Sew the edges of the two pieces of fabric together, making sure not to sew the pillows' hole closed.
5. Turn the pillowcase inside out: Put your pillow in and done. (Finish)

Sewing a Picnic Blanket

Supplies:

- Measuring tape
- Fabric chalk
- Cotton batting (Optional)
- Fabric
- Rotary cutter or sewing scissors
- Clamps or a heavy object (Optional)
- Bias tape
- Thread
- Sewing Machine
- Needle (Optional)
- Sewing pins

Picnic Blanket Making Process

1. Mark Your dimensions: using fabric chalk, mark your measurements on the fabric, use a heavy object or a clap to keep the material taut.
2. Repeat the process: Follow the same steps for the second layer of fabric; these will be sewn together after they have been cut out.
3. Cut the fabric: Using a rotary cutter or a pair of sewing scissors to carve clean lines.
4. Spread the cotton batting: If you're filling your blanket with padding, add the padding to the center of the fabric, making sure that it is flush with the sides. You can add as much padding as you would like; the choice is entirely up to you.
5. Set your two layers on top of each other: Once you have lined your corners up, place sewing pins in each corner to secure the fabric in place (You can fold each edge over itself before pinning if you'd like a cleaner edge).
6. Stitch the edges: Stitch the edges with a strong thread that has been run through your sewing machine. Ensure that the speed is set to the lowest setting.
7. Sew additional seams: Sew an additional seam down the middle if you have added padding.
8. Remove the pins: Once you have finished sewing, the pins can be removed, ensuring that the fabric stays in place whilst sewing. (Finish)

Tapestry

When you think of tapestry, you probably automatically think of weaving with a loom; you wouldn't be totally wrong in your assumptions; however, you wouldn't be completely right either. When it comes to distinguishing tapestry weaving from standard weaving, there are differences and similarities.

The main difference is in the threads and the number of forms they can take. That being said, with weaving, you use warp (vertical) threads and weft (horizontal) threads as opposed to weft-faced threads used in tapestry. What this insinuates is that the horizontal threads (wefts) are distinguishable whilst the warp (vertical) threads are not.

Moon Phase Wall Art

Supplies:

- Rolling pin
- Round cookie cutter
- Drill

- String
- Superglue
- Skewer
- Ten pieces of square dowel

Wall Art Crafting Process

1. Roll your clay: Roll Your clay to a thickness of about ¼ of an inch/ 0.6 cm.
2. Cut out your circles: Cut out seven 2-3 inches/ 5-7 cm circles using your cookie cutter.
3. Use the cookie cutter or knife: Using the cookie cutter or knife, cut out the moon's phases.
4. Smooth out the edges and use a skewer: Using your finger, smooth out the edges, then proceed to use the skewer to poke a hole on top of each of the moon's phases where the string will go.
5. Let it dry: Let the clay sit and dry.
6. Drill holes in the Dowel: Drill seven evenly spaced small holes in the dowel.
7. Cut the string: Cut three 40 inch/ 101.5 cm strings and a single piece of 26 inch/ 66 cm string.
8. Fold the string: Take three pieces of 40 inch/ 101.5 cm string and fold them in half, fold about 2 inches/ 5 cm down on top of the 26 inch/ 66 cm string. Now take all four loops created with the fold and make a knot. This is what your wall art will be hanging from.
9. Trim the excess: Trim the string from the short end that had been created when knotting the 26 inch/ 66 cm string.
10. Thread the string: thread each string through a hole in the dowel and tie a knot underneath (make sure that the knots are all even)
11. Trim the ends: Trim the ends of the string to create a V shape.
12. When the clay is dry: If the clay is dry, dab glue into each of the holes made with the skewer and slide the string inside, let sit to dry. (Finish)

Beach Blanket Tapestry

Supplies:

- Yarn or twine
- Iron (Only needed if your using stitch witchery)
- 2x3 Woven rugs
- Stitch witchery or a thread and needle if your rug is too thick
- Dowel rod

How to Make a Woven Beach Blanket

1. Cut the Dowel rod: Start by cutting the dowel rod; make sure that the dowel is a couple of inches or centimeters longer than what you are weaving.
2. Flip the rugs over: Place the dowel where it needs to go, then add a stitch witch underneath the Dowel rod.
3. Make use of the iron: Run the iron over the top until the two pieces have been bonded (If you have a thick rug, you may need to use a needle and thread).
4. Use a piece of yarn: Tie a piece of yarn down to each side of the dowel and cut off any excess material.
5. Use an extra bit of yarn: Use an additional piece of yarn and weave through a hole in the brass and make a weaving opening in the rug. (This particular Woven wall hanging can be taken off and used as a beach blanket). (Finish)

Bedspread Tapestry

Supplies:

- Pins
- White thread
- All-purpose glue
- Sewing machine
- White pom poms
- Gold tube bead (optional)
- Cotton table runner
- 200g of white chunky wool

How to Make a Bedspread

1. Iron the table runner: Begin by ironing the table runner smooth and then folding the whole thing in half.
2. Thread the sewing machine: Thread your sewing machine with the white thread and sew down both sides of the runner.
3. Sew across: Sew across through the ironed fold at the bottom to secure the tasseled edge.
4. Sew meshed parts: Sew each meshed piece to the underside.
5. Wool fringing: Take wool sections and fold them over 4-5 times, then grab a shorter piece of wool and tie a knot around the top. Doing so forms a little tassel. You will need to do this repeatedly until you form two lines with small spaces in between each.
6. Take your two lines of tassels: You will need to take both lines and sew them with the tops hidden underneath the tassels.
7. Trim the fringing: Trim the fringing of the wool to the lengths desired or short enough to make space for some pom poms.
8. Sew the pom-poms: Sew the pom-poms in two rows above the cotton mesh parts of the table runner. However, these can be glued if you don't own a sewing machine.
9. Use some leftover wool: Cut strips to loop over and pin this evenly, sew them together by adding a line of stitching all the way along the top
10. Add some contrast (Optional): Slides some beads onto the tassels spacing them evenly whilst tying a knot under each of them. (Finish)

Photo Backdrop

Supplies:

- Iron
- Freezer paper
- Palmistry printables (8,5x11x17)
- Muslin (Or any different type of fabric)
- Fabric glue and sewing supplies
- Rope
- Fringe trim
- Wood Dowel

How to Make a Photo Backdrop

1. Iron the freezer paper: Iron the freezer paper to the fabric, ensuring that the waxy side is touching the material.
2. Cut the freezer paper: Cut the freezer paper and fabric to the print size.
3. Feed it into your printer: If you are unsure as to which side, draw an arrow on a standard piece of paper and see how it goes through the printer. Let this dry for 5-10 minutes.
4. Prevent Fraying: to prevent fraying, attach the trim to the, you can add a small layer of fabric glue along the ends of the tapestry or sew everything down.
5. Add rope: Add some rope to the ends of the tapestry. (Finish)

Weaving

Weaving can be a fun, calming, and soothing activity for you and the whole family, children included. Why weaving, you may ask? Weaving has been linked to improved development of fine motor skills like hand-eye coordination, literacy, numeracy, language skills as well as problem-solving in children and adults. Moreover, weaving is a quiet and calming activity that allows individuals to express their creativity no matter the material.

Woven Necklace

Supplies:

- 4 inches/ 10 cm of copper wire
- Cotton twine
- Necklace chain (At desired length)
- Yarn (Optional)
- Twelve stone beads
- Thick cardboard measuring about 5 inches/12.7 cm x 7 inches/17.7 cm
- Tapestry needle for weaving

- Thread in coordinating colors
- Hand-sewing needle for threading through the stones

How to Weave a Necklace

1. Cut the cardboard: Measure out about 5 inches/12.7 cm x 7 inches/17.7 cm and wrap your twine around it so that you have ten rows on the front side. Tie your two ends into a knot on the backside; this is your warp.
2. Cut a second piece: cut a second piece of thread, twine, or yarn if you want a different color through your tapestry needle. This is called a "Weft." Start from the right under the second warp row. Next, continue going over and under with your needle until you get to the left side. Next, wrap around the warp and weave over and under back to the right side; this should be the opposite row you just did.
3. Pull your twine: When you pull your string through each new row, go up at a slight angle and then down so that you get a hill shape in the middle, then pull it down gently in the center of the hill so that it lays flat. Pull the rest of the row down to lay flat against the previous row. Making the hill gives you a little bit of slack so that you are not making it tighter and tighter as you go along (This will help you avoid the hourglass shape).
4. Press your row flat: Continue going back and forth, over and under, or until your twine has almost run out.
5. End the twine: End the twine with three tails tucked under the warp.
6. Keep weaving: Keep weaving until you reach the desired length. You'll need a little space at the top and bottom for your warp strands (These will be required to tie the knot).
7. Flip the cardboard over: Flip the cardboard loom over to the backside. Next, cut your warp thread to about 1 inch/ 2.5 cm from the top.
8. Gently re-thread: Re-thread the starting length of twine and stitch vertically through a few rows of weaving. Repeat this with the end piece of yarn as well. You can do this to all the loose ends or double-knot the ones that are near each other.
9. Wrap nine strands; however, ten is advised: Making ten allows you to have an even amount to tie off. Tie a double-knot between

every two warp threads along the top and bottom. This helps lock in your weaving.
10. Fold the top knots: Take your thread and sewing needle and fold the top knots back to the backside. Make sure you're careful so that you do not stitch all the way through your weaving.
11. Stitch the stones: Stitch the stones in place using the same needle and thread. You can do two rows of six; however, this can be easily adjusted.
12. Thread the chain: Thread the chain through the copper pipe and cut another twine thread about 2 inches/ 5 cm long. Stitch it through one corner of your necklace under the double-knotted warp. Continue stitching until you have made it to the other side. (Finish)

Place Mats

Supplies:

- Scissors
- Marker
- Embroidery needle (You can use a normal needle and black thread)
- Cardboard piece 14 inches/ 35.5 cm x 14 inches/ 35.5 cm
- Black embroidery thread
- Macrame cotton cord

How to Make a Place Mat

1. Make a knot: First, tie a knot at the end of the first cord, start in the center and weave in a spiral. Make sure to alternate the thread so that it hides the knots underneath the weaving. Once you reach the end of the first cord, knot it, and repeat the process until all your cords have been used. Trim the last cord to match up with one of the ends of the embroidery threads and tie a knot.
2. Cut the cardboard: Cut the cardboard, leaving a 2 inches/5 cm-3 inches/7 cm tail on each piece. Wrap each tail around the closest cord and tie in a knot to secure it.
3. Take the embroidery: Wrap it several times around the four outer cords at the spot where your final cord ended, covering the knot.

Repeat this for every other area where the embroidery thread is located.
4. Make some tassels: Make eight small tassels and attach these to the placemat with regular black thread, or embroidery thread, and a large needle. (Finish)

DIY Woven Bag

Supplies:

- 3-4 Used dog food bags
- Sewing machine
- Scissors
- Square frame
- Tape
- Fabric for lining
- Measuring tape
- Straight pins

How to Weave a Bag

1. Tape the strips to a square frame: Tape down both ends and place the strips as close as you can without overlapping
2. Weaving: You can now start weaving move strips in and out of the first set of strips; this is called "Weft" weaving.
3. Remove the weaving from inside the frame: Tape the woven strips closed and cut the excess off.
4. Sew the strips: This step ensures that the weaving stays in place when you turn it inside out; when you are done sewing the edges, you can cut off the outside edges that have tape on them.
5. Construct the bag: Cut the piece of fabric to the exact size of lining, fold the seaming in half and stitch up the side seams. In the bottom corner, sew across, creating corners do the same with the lining. Place the lining inside the bag; next, pin the lining to the bag. Matching up the side seams, cut strips of plastic for the binding and handles. Bind the top edges.

Woven Tea Towel (Warp, Plain Weave)

Supplies:

- Main Yarn
- Contrast Yarn
- Cricket Loom

How to Weave a Tea Towel

1. Leave a tail: Leave a 36 inch/ 91 cm tail of main yarn at the beginning.
2. Main Yarn: Weave 16 rows
3. Contrast Yarn: Weave three rows
4. Main Yarn: Weave seven rows
5. Contrast Yarn Weave 3 rows
6. Main Yarn: Weave 18½ inches
7. Contrast Yarn: Weave 3
8. Main yarn: Weave 7
9. Contrast Yarn: Weave 15
10. Main Yarn: Weave 7
11. Contrast Yarn: Weave 3
12. Main Yarn: Weave 16
13. Cut both yarns: Cut both yarns, leaving a 36-inch tail of Main Yarn
14. Hemstitch: Finish both ends with a hemstitch (Finish)

Woodworking

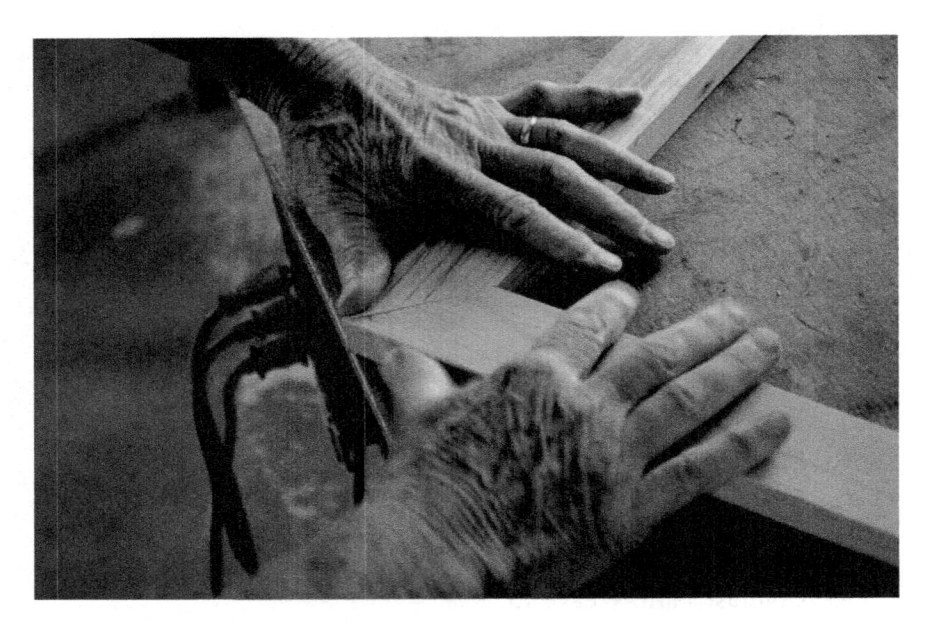

Did you know that woodworking has health benefits? If not, you will be surprised to learn that as a hobby, it can boost your mood and improve your mental sharpness. By partaking in woodworking, you are unknowingly producing serotonin, the chemical in your brain that enables you to feel happy and content. Moreso, when you have completed a task, you will be filled with a sense of completion and pride which is also a big mood booster.

Making a Bench

Equipment:

- Old Ikea cupboard
- Four screw-in feet
- Drill
- Long cushion
- Paint of your color (Optional)
- Strips of velcro

How to Build a Bench

1. Gather materials: gather all the material that you will need.
2. Turn the old Bookshelf/cupboard onto its side: Drill four holes of the correct length into the cupboard/bookshelf.
3. Screw in the legs: Take your four legs and screw them into the holes you have drilled. Make sure that the holes were drilled on each corner of the table/cupboard.
4. Turn the table: Turn the table so that the feet are flat on the ground.
5. Add cushions: Add your cushion to the base of the bench
6. Add velcro: Add two strips of velcro, one underneath the cushion and one at the base of the bench, in order to stick the cushion down.
7. Paint: Paint the bench with a color that you would like, maybe something rustic perhaps the choice is up to you, and this is entirely optional. (Finish)

Making an Easel

Equipment:

- Buy three pieces of wood that are about 2.4m/7.9ft long
- Measuring tape
- Screws
- Hinge
- Dowels
- Saw
- Hammer and drill (Optional)
- Rope

How to Make an Easel

1. Cut and measure the wood: The wood should be cut into two pieces that are 5.9ft/1.8 m long (MainLeg), one piece that is 4.9ft/1.5 m long (Back leg), one piece that is 27inches/68 cm long (Cross piece), one piece that is 9.1 inches/21 cm long (Cross piece)

2. Layout in a capital A shape: layout the two longest pieces of wood so that it forms an A, then place the 27inch/68 cm down so that it forms the horizontal line in the middle of the "A."
3. Secure and cut: Drill three screws into each side of the 21inch/68 cm to secure it to the 5.9ft/1.8 m piece. You can always utilize a hammer and nails if you don't have a drill.
4. Attach the 9,1inch/23 cm piece to the top of the "A": Flip the "A" frame over carefully and attach the 9.1inch/21 cm to the wooden frame using a drill or hammer.
5. Attach a hinge: Secure a hinge to the 4.9ft/1.5 m piece below with screws
6. Drill a hole: Drill the hole through the center of the 27inch/68 cm pieces of wood and the back leg. Thread the rope through each hole and knot both ends. This will provide extra support.
7. Drill Dowel holes at 0.59inch/1.5 cm: Starting at 27inch on the horizontal bar, drill the holes on both o.o59ft/1.8 cm pieces.
8. Place the Dowels: Place the dowels into the holes and a cross member on top. The cross-member should be just slightly wider than the frame.
9. Stand it up: Stand the Easel upon its two main legs and get to work. (Finish)

Making a Mini Pallet Coaster

Equipmnet:

- Pen/pencil
- Sandpaper
- Ruler
- 7 Craft sticks
- Scissors or craft blade
- Silver permanent marker (Optional)
- Acrylic tape, washi tape, and black coffee (Optional)
- 3.8 inches /9.7 cm thick balsa wooden stick (or any wood of your choice)
- Hot glue gun

How to Make a Wooden Coaster

1. Cut the craft sticks: Cut seven craft sticks into 4inch/10 cm lengths. Take your pen/pencil and off the rounded ends of each craft stick. (Should be 4 inch/10 cm long) Cut along the markers using scissors or a blade.
2. Cut the balsa wood: Cut the balsa wood into three 4 inch/10 cm smaller sticks. (Sides and middle of pallet)
3. Sand and cut ends: Sand and cut the ends smooth. (Optional).
4. Stain the craft sticks: Stain the craft sticks with coffee by placing all of your sticks into a container and leaving them to sit in there for 5 minutes. Your sticks should be dried thoroughly before moving on; if you'd like a different pattern, you can always cover the sticks with washi tape or paint them with acrylic paint.
5. Arrange the sticks: Arrange the balsa sticks to form the number !!!
6. Hot glue: Utilize a hot glue gun and stick the sticks horizontally across the balsa wood sticks.
7. Mark: Mark tiny naily using a silver marker by simply adding two dots at each end of the craft sticks. (Finish)

Making a Faucet Coat Hanger

Supplies:

- Two nails
- 2 Screw on faucets
- Piece of wood
- Sandpaper
- Drill
- Saw
- One long wall nail
- Varnish

How to Make a Faucet Coat Hanger

1. Buy your faucet and wood: Aquire your two faucets and wood from your local DIY store.
2. Sand your wood: Sand your wood down and measure out your two drill hole spaces evenly.

3. Screw-in: Screw your faucet into the wood, ensuring they are tightly in place.
4. Varnish: Once you are happy with your coat hanger, you can varnish it down. This will leave your wood looking more vibrant (Optional). (Finish)

Art Therapy

Many individuals of all ages have turned to art therapy in recent years to improve sensorimotor and cognitive functions. As a hobby, research suggests it can improve communication, reduce feelings of isolation and improve concentration. Moreover, it has also been linked to increases in confidence, self-awareness, and self-esteem in all aspects of life. So, why not give it a try. You might even be pleasantly surprised.

Flower Art

Supplies:

- Plastic plate
- Acrylic paint colors of your choosing
- Old tree stump
- Long nail
- Hammer
- Scissors

How to Make Flower Art

1. Design: Design your flower and begin choosing the colors that you would like to use.
2. Cut: Cut your plastic plate to the shape of the flower that you'd like to create.
3. Find a stump: Find an old tree stump; this will be the stem of your new flower art. Simply place the flower at the top of the stump (Not on top) and then hammer it in with the nail and hammer.

Portrait Painting

Supplies:

- Easel
- Paintbrushes or stencils
- Canvas paper

How to Make a Portrait Painting

1. Find a picture: Find a picture of yourself or a friend and use this to draw your portrait painting.
2. Canvas paper: Set up the easel with the canvas paper.
3. Begin: Start drawing/painting your portrait into the canvas. (Finish)

Finger Painting

Supplies:

- Paint of your choosing
- Paper or a canvas

How to Create a Finger Painting

1. Get your paint and paper: Get your paint sandpaper ready this will be the very first thing that you will do
2. Idea in mind: Have a fundamental concept in mind as to what you would like to paint or perhaps do a little research.

3. Paint: Start painting and use your fingers; your fingers will be used instead of a paintbrush. (Finish)

Drawing/Doodling

Supplies:

- Pen/pencil
- Paper/canvas
- Easel

How to Start Drawing

1. Gather your materials: Gather all the material that you will need, such as your pen/pencil and paper/canvas this is all you will need unless you have an easel which you can use,
2. Have an idea: Have a basic idea as to what you would like to doodle/draw.
3. Start drawing: Begin drawing something; anything is fine, let your mind run rampant. (Finish)

Pottery

In recent years pottery has come into the spotlight for its ability to increase optimistic outlook. How, you may be wondering? Well, pottery enables improvements in flow and spontaneity. What does this mean exactly? This means that pottery provides an outlet for those who are grieving (and those who are not.) Specifically speaking, it provides them with an outlet for self-expression, boosting confidence and self-esteem, as well as a means of self-identification.

Vase with Handles

Material:

- Bowl of water
- Air-dry clay
- Rolling pin
- Scalpel or specialized clay tool
- Plastic bottle or any other small container
- Baking soda and acrylic paint if you'd like to paint the vase

How to Make a Vase with Handles

1. Take a chunk: Take a lump of clay and roll it out to roughly 0.8 inches/ 2 cm thick, making sure that it's slightly taller than your bottle.
2. Wrap: Wrap the clay around the bottle.
3. Close the gap: Using some water, wet your fingertips and gently close any gaps around the vase.
4. Cut: Cut two slits into the vase at the top. This will be for the handles.
5. Press: Press the top section into the bottleneck and again use water to smooth the vase and close any gaps.
6. Roll separate clay: Roll another individual ball of clay; this will be used for the bottom of the vase.
7. Trim: Trim around the edges of the clay leaving just enough to close it off.
8. Join the clay: Press the clay to join it, working all your way around the bottom of the vase (use water if necessary).
9. Roll a cylinder: Roll A cylinder of clay that will be used for the handles. Make sure that it is long enough as this piece will be cut in half.
10. Join: Join in the same way that you did when making the bottom of your clay case.
11. Let it dry: Let the clay sit, and dry, usually the packaging that the clay comes with has the estimated time frame of how long the Air dry clay will take to dry. (Finish)

Clay Plate (Slab Technique)

Supplies:

- Uncoated paper plates
- Strips of wood (Optional)
- Cut-off wire
- Rolling pin
- Needle tool
- Sponge
- Clay with sand r grog in it to reduce warping

How to Make a Clay Plate

1. Get your clay: Throw out a ten by ten cm (4 by 4 inch) piece of clay, lift and throw the clay seven times. Doing this will help remove any air bubbles in the clay.
2. Place your strips: Place your wooden strips on the table to help create an even layer of clay.
3. Roll: Roll the clay out with the rolling pin. Suppose you are using the wooden piece roll part of the pin on them.
4. Create surface: Create a smooth surface by placing the clay on a piece of paper or baker's paper. Next, smooth out both sides of the clay with something flat.
5. Trace: Tracing around an uncoated plate will give you the shape of the plate, and a needle tool can be used during this process.
6. Remove the extra: Remove the excess clay from your plate using the needle tool or a blade.
7. Leave to dry: Let the dish sit and dry the packaging will tell you as to how long you should wait. (Finish)

Clay Mug

Supplies:

- Bow/container with water
- Clay crafting tools
- Clay
- Rolling pin

How to Make a Clay Mug

1. Roll your clay: Roll your clay to the desired length and width you would like.
2. Smooth the clay: Smooth out the clay; you can use any item that works well for smoothing.
3. Cut: Cut out your slab of clay to the width and length that you require.
4. Score: Score the borders. This will make the clay more susceptible to sticking.
5. Unite the borders: Use a little water to combine the borders.
6. Smooth: Smooth out the borders; the seam and the outside of the cup should be smooth.
7. Make the bottom: Position the cup on top of the clay and cut off the excess, score the bottom of the borders, and wet them.
8. Unite the bottom: attach the bottom with a bit of water. Remember that the clay might become hard while working, so wet your sponge and apply a little water while you work to keep the clay pliable.
9. Drying: Let the clay dry until fully hardened. You can opt to paint your cup using acrylic paint. Just ensure that the paint is waterproof and is fully set before use. (Finish)

Clay Planter

Supplies:

- Sandpaper
- Paper towel
- Clay tool for scoring
- Clay tool for mixing and applying slip
- Pliers
- Bowl
- Sponge
- Ruler
- Knife
- Rolling ping
- Air-dry clay

How to Make a Clay Planter

1. Roll your clay: Roll out your clay to the desired shape and form. Make sure that you use enough clay and have the correct measurements for your design.
2. Design a detail: Design a detail by bending a paperclip into the shape of a "U" or any other shape that you desire.
3. Make it smooth: Gently rub a wet sponge across the clay to smooth out any rough edges.
4. Score the clay: Score the clay so that when you join the sides, it ensures that your planter is held in place firmly.
5. Put it all together: Once you have shaped, smoothed, and scored your planter, join all the pieces together.
6. Let it dry: Let the clay sit and dry until it has hardened; you can paint your planter after this. Depending on where it will be used indoors or out, make sure that the paint you buy is waterproof, as some paints can be harmful to your succulents if it runs into the soil.

Mind and Body

When you think of your mind and body, do you think of them together or as opposing forces? Having a perfect mind and body balance is crucial to feeling stress-free and relaxed not only at home but at work and in social instances too. By looking after your mind and your body as a unit instead of separately, you will be more open to creating and exploring your own unique mind and body harmony.

Candle Making

Candle making might sound like a challenging craft, but it does not depend on what method you go for. To make this a little more straightforward for you, we will be discussing the melt and pour method. Also known as melt and pour waxes. Like soap, candles can also come in the form of melt and pour varieties.

These candles only need to be heated to approximately 151 F/70 C before pouring the wax into your desired shape or form. Remember to make sure your wax has cooled to this temperature to ensure a safe candle-making process.

There are many varying blends that these waxes can come in depending on the company you source your wax from. Make sure you research the wax you'd like to buy first. You don't want to buy something you're not going to use.

Tools and Safety Equipment

Fire Extinguisher

Since you will be working with wax, a flammable substance composed of many oils, you will need to buy a dry chemical (ABC) type fire extinguisher. This ensures you are fully prepared in case any fire breaks out. It's important to remember that you must never throw water onto a wax fire as this can cause the wax to splash on you; this can harm yourself and or others.

Mold Sealer

Mould sealer will be vital if you use a mold; otherwise, you most likely won't need it. They can acquire them from your local DIY store, art and craft stores, or online. The mold will be used to block the hole you made in order to thread your wick through the base of the mold.

Candle Wax

Candle wax can be either artificial or natural in nature. As you move forward on your journey as a candle maker, it will be beneficial for you to know the difference between the two. Natural waxes are sustainable, biodegradable, and burn longer than artificial wax. This is easier to clean up too. Unfortunately, these are hard to acquire, even at your local DIY or craft stores. Purchasing these online would theoretically be your best option.

Clothespins

This is the best item to use as a novice candle maker when it comes to setting your wick as they are cost affordable and dependable when it comes to cable making. You can also use them as multi-wick applications, containers, and wide diameter jars.

It's important to remember that you will need to have self-restraint when centering your wick. On another note, when it comes to clothespins, you can also purchase a wick bar if you are concerned about placing your wick in the middle.

Protective Masks

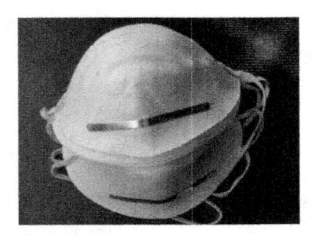

When working with candles mainly made from paraffin, It's crucial to ensure your workspace is thoroughly ventilated. This is to prevent the unwanted inhaling of toxic fumes during the melting of wax or adding of fragrance oil during the candle-making process. By wearing a mask, you will considerably reduce the intake of harmful chemicals into your body.

Drill

To ensure drilling the holes into your mold base, you will need an awl or drill. So ensuring you have either of the two items will make the candle-making process go a whole lot easier.

Candle Wicks

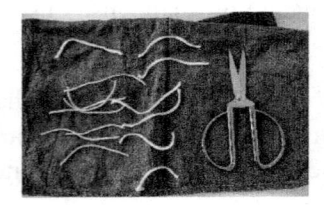

There are four kinds of basic candle wicks available on the market today, and choosing the correct wick can be a tedious process. Many choices come into play when you are selecting your candlewick. These factors include fragrance load, type of wax dye, type of wax you will be using, and container diameter.

Kitchen Scale

This item is crucial to cable making as you will need to measure everything from wax to essential oils. If you're genuinely serious about the craft, invest in a scale.

Glass Measuring Cup

It will be beneficial to have a glass measuring cup as you will need to melt and stir the fragrances or dyes into the wax. Glass measuring cups can come in many various sizes and should be as large as 765 g/27 oz. These glass measuring cups provide easier cleaning.

Glass Thermometer

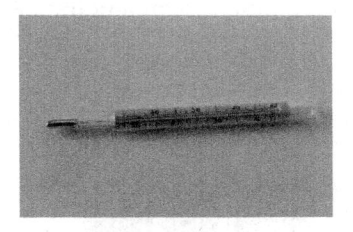

A glass thermometer will be crucial when gauging the temperature of your wax accurately as it goes through the heating and cooling stages. You will need to keep up-to-date with the different stages in the cable-making process as follows.

The solid should melt down into a liquid wax; this liquid wax+Essential fragrance oils = Fragrance + solid wax (finished candle). To achieve the necessary heat required in the candle-making process, you will have to have a glass thermometer at the very least.

If you can cough up a little bit more, then get yourself a handheld infrared heat gun; this device uses infrared light rays that bounce off the surface of the wax to give an accurate temperature.

Essential Oils (Optional)

When it comes to scenting your candles, the possibilities are endless, and it's beneficial to get your essential oils and fragrances from a reliable source that you trust. It's vital to keep in mind that many suppliers sell synthetic, low-quality, or watered-down oils on the market. So for the best possible outcome, do a little research beforehand.

Tape Measure

The tape measure will be indispensable as you will need to measure the height and diameter of your mold or container for your candle. This ensures your wick sits at the appropriate height.

Containers

The candle-making journey cannot come to an end until the way has been poured into its mold. When it comes to molds, you can buy a specific mold to pour your wax into, or you can use any ordinary container that will be able to handle the heat well.

These molds can include mason jars, eggshells, metal tins, and perhaps old mugs and old clay garden pots. You can certainly use any mold as long as it's fire and heatproof. Your mold size will all depend on how much wax you will be melting down and the desired look you are going for.

In addition to the other container, you can also use a cardboard box coated with vegetable oil to create your molds at home if you're running on a tight budget. Wax is a highly flammable material, so it's crucial to ensure that what you pour your wax into is heat resistant.

Rubber gloves

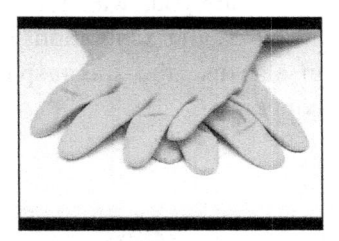

To ensure a safe candle-making journey, make sure you have a pair of long protective rubber gloves or wear a shirt that has long sleeves to match the short gloves. Wearing a pair of safety gloves protects the hands from any hot or potent oils that can come into contact with the skin on your hands.

Make sure that the gloves you've acquired are chemically resistant to protect your skins from coming into contact with potent fragrances or essential oils.

Measuring Spoons

To ensure that your candles are made correctly, it's of the utmost importance for you to measure out your ingredients to the exact weight required by that set recipe. By doing so, you can precisely measure the ingredients before you begin making your candle.

Spoons or Spatulas for Mixing

You will require this tool to stir your wax for even melting, mixing in fragrances or color, as well as the separation of any large chunks of unmelted wax. You can also use the spoon/spatula to scrape off any leftover wax inside the container.

Safety Glasses

Protecting your eyes is essential when it comes to candle-making, more so than your skin but still of equal importance. Hot wax can cause irreparable damage to your eyes, especially if you're not wearing any protection.

That's why it's crucial to wear safety glasses to prevent any backsplash from reaching your eyes. Likewise, you will have to make sure your glasses are chemically resistant.

Double Boiler

For this specific method, a glass-measuring cup will work best to make sure that the glass-measuring cup can handle repeated temperature fluctuations. This is one of the most low-risk methods when heating candle wax in candle-making.

The only problem with this is that it takes longer for the wax to melt. However, this ensures your wax doesn't burn.

Wax Additives (Optional)

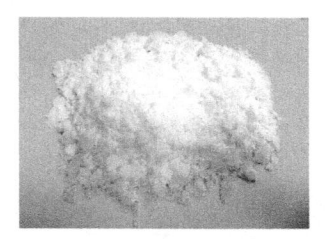

As the word may suggest, these additives are artificial, and almost all candle-makers will opt for a more natural alternative over artificial ones. These candles are generally fine; just keep in mind that along your journey, you might find that only an additive may be able to fix your problem.

Candle or Wax Dye (Optional)

You can find candle dye in either solid, liquid, or flake form in an array of colors to suit your design needs. Each of these dyes is unique in its application methods and can be purchased at your local DIY and arts and craft stores and online with retailers such as Amazon.

For starters, liquid dye is combined with melted wax and has to be combined evenly throughout your mixture to ensure the dye is blended correctly. This provides a richer color to your finished candle. Solid dyes are made up of whole color segments (cut into smaller pieces) and mixed into your melted wax.

Lastly, wax flakes are mixed in with the melted wax for even distribution. These flake dyes and solids will leave your candle with a more pastel and muted shade. It's of great importance to remember that soy wax doesn't necessarily combine well with most dyes and will more than often produce a muted shade.

These waxes will generally come with instructions from the manufacturer, and it is up to you as the candle-maker to follow the steps accordingly.

Candlewick Tabs

Candle Wicks can be easily identified as small circle metal discs that can be fixed and secured to the candle to ensure the correct placement of the candlewick inside. You can use a little hot glue or melted wax, preferably to secure the wick to the bottom of the container or mold. Once attached you can pour the remaining wax placing the wick in the center of the clothespin or bar to solidify and cool down.

Container Candles

These types of candles are specifically made to sit within a jar, metal tin, or glass container with or without the lid. These candles cannot stand on their own and are often made from softer wax types like paraffin blends, paraffin, soy, and palm wax.

Container candles can also be made with beeswax; however, this will require multiple or larger wicks to burn correctly. If your candle doesn't stick to the container properly, it can cause the candle to end up having a candle that looks like it has wax spots.

This happens more often when you use pillar waxes inside a container; these container waxes can come in many different types like granulated, slab, and even flake forms.

How to Make a Basic Container Candle?

Step One: Gather All Equipment

It's essential to gather all the material you will need to make the candle beforehand, and it's highly recommended you lay down wax paper over your work surface.

Step Two: Preheat Your Oven

You should preheat your oven to precisely 65-76 C/150-170 F or the lowest temperature available for your container. Place your containers onto a baking tray and insert them in the oven. This will prevent any breaks or cracks from forming and avoid possible jump lines.

Step Three: Weighing Your Wax Accordingly

Weigh out the precise amount of wax you will need to fill your containers; keep in mind that 3 lbs/1.4 kgs of wax are the equivalent to 3.5 lbs/1.6 kgs of water.

Step Four: Heating Your Wax

The next step will be to heat your wax in your double boiler at a temperature of 76-82 C/170-180 F or at medium heat, as the water doesn't necessarily need to be at a boil to melt the wax. It's crucial to keep checking the temperature of your wax as you do not want it to get too hot.

Step Five: Measuring Your Essential Oils Or Fragrances

It's important to measure out your essential oils and fragrances. Once this has been done, you can add them to your wax. Make sure that the wax has been cooled to the appropriate temperature. Although, the standard practice for essential oils or fragrances is 1 lb/454 g of wax per every 1 oz/28.3 g of scent.

Step Six: Measuring and Adding Your Dyes

Once the other steps have been followed accordingly, you can measure and add your dye to your wax mixture. You must mix the dye until thoroughly combined, but it is advised not to overuse the amount of color you put in as you cannot remove it once the dye has been added.

Step Seven: Test Your Colours

Test the color using white paper strips. If you are unimpressed with the color, you can always add more just keep in mind that once the dye has been added, it can't be taken out.

Step Eight: Mixing Your Ingredients

You can now mix your ingredients for about 2-3 minutes, ensuring the ingredients are combined evenly throughout your mixture. If oily residue is still present on the surface of your mixture, you will have to continue mixing until it has thoroughly been incorporated into your mixture.

Step Nine: Setting Your Wick

Now that the other steps are complete, you can set your wick onto the bottom of the mold or container using a wick sticker or heat-resistant glue.

Step Ten: Pouring in Your Melted Wax

Once you have centered your wick, you can then begin to pour in your melted wax until it fills the widest part of your mold or container. Do not rush after pouring your wax; this can lead to backsplashes; this could get onto your clothes or skin and leave dried wax on the inside of your container. Not only will this cause injury, but it can also lead to your candle having air pockets on the surface.

Step Eleven: Securing Your Wick

In this next step, you will need to secure your wick. You can use either a metal skewer, clothes peg, or a wick bar. You can achieve this by pulling the wick gently before either wrapping it around the metal skewer or clothespin or slotting it into a wick bar. This must be done before placing it onto the rim of the container. You can now set the mold aside to cool, be careful not to bump the mixture or move it unnecessarily.

Step Twelve: Removing the Candle

Now that the candle has cooled completely, you can remove the wick holder. You might notice that a small indent has appeared around the open section of your wick. Worry not; this is an easy fix; simply pour a little melted wax into the cavity to even and fill it out.

Step Thirteen: Trimming Your Wick

You can now trim your wick to about 0.6cm or ¼ of an inch long or however long you desire it for your decorative purposes. Make sure not to cut your wick too short, as this can cause your candle to not burn properly. If desired, you can also add the lid back onto the jar.

Step Fourteen: Safety First

As an added precaution, you can add warning labels to the base of your candle or container, which will be beneficial to you and or your business.

Soap Making

Soap making can also sound like a complex craft, but in reality, it can become much simpler depending on what method you use. We will also discuss the melt and pour method for soap making, as it's one of the simpler forms of soap making.

Otherwise known as soap casting, the heat and pour method is by far the easiest. All you are required to do is melt the premade soap base of your choice and add any extras like herbs, oils, etc.

Unfortunately, the only downside to this particular method is that you have a few limitations as to what you can use due to the fact you're using someone else's product.

Safety Gear and Equipment Needed

Measuring Cup:

It's essential to always ensure that you have a measuring cup when making soap. This enables you to precisely and accurately measure out the required ingredients. Ensure that you have the correct number of measuring cups before you start making your soap.

Thermometer:

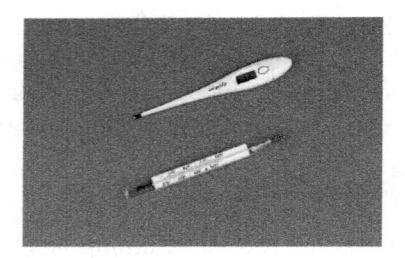

Ensuring you have a thermometer nearby when you are making your soap is crucial in order to correctly gauge the temperature of the lye water properly and the oils for your soap solution.

Safety Goggles:

It's always beneficial to keep a pair of safety goggles around. Not only will the goggles protect you from potential splashes that could possibly cause irreparable damage to your eyes, but also it's a smart idea. It's important to note that soap that has not undergone saponification can be just as corrosive as lye itself.

Non-Metal Spoons and Spatulas:

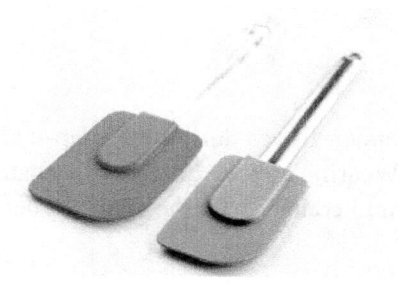

Lye is an incredibly corrosive material; that's why it's crucial that what you mix your soap solution with is non-metal. The reason it's essential to keep this in mind when making your soap is that your spatula or spoon, if you're using one, can melt along with your solution. Ideally, you will use a wooden spoon when mixing and plastic ones to scrape out any leftover soap inside the pot. This is why it's a good idea to check beforehand if your spatula is heat resistant.

Non-metal Dishes or Crock-Pots:

In the same scenario, it's a wise idea to use non-metal dishes or crock-pots when cooking your soap. You can always substitute your non-metal dishes or crock-pots for plastic or stainless steel ones. It would be a great idea to have a larger size pot to mix all your ingredients instead of doing it in smaller batches.

Rubber Gloves:

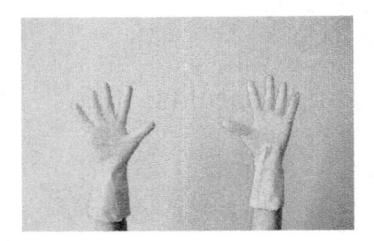

Remember to wear rubber gloves during the soap-making process as lye is highly corrosive. Wearing rubber gloves will ensure that no harmful chemicals will come into contact with the skin on your hands.

Scales:

Soap making is all about chemistry and measuring your ingredients accurately. To begin making your soap, you will need to have a weight-sensitive scale in order to precisely measure the oils and dyes you will be using, ingredients, and weight of the lye. There are three different scales to choose from; however, it's important to remember to select a ranking that can handle what you'll be utilizing it for.

Spring Scale:

This is known as one of those scales that would be in your best interest to stay away from.

Digital/Electronic Scale:

If you're thoroughly interested in soap making, then this scale is the perfect choice for you. A digital scale can measure ingredients more precisely than an average scale, and that's exactly what an aspiring soap maker is looking for.

Battery Scale:

This scale is not highly recommended as it can run out of battery during the soap-making process.

How to Choose the Right Scale?

When choosing the scale that will suit your needs its important to consider the following tips:

- It should have a large enough reading panel.
- It shouldn't be a spring scale.
- The platforms size
- It comes with an AC adapter

- The weight of your soap batch sizes
- Should read in grams and ounces
- Includes the Tare function; this is crucial

The Rebatching Method for Soap Making

This method, otherwise known as the hand milling method, is by far one of the most straightforward soap-making processes. This means even a novice soap maker can use this method as it's one of the most cost-effective and shortest methods out of all the other soap-making processes.

Simply put, the rebatch method is taking failed or old batches of soap as long as there aren't any variations in the lye and fats in the solution and recycling them into new soap. This way uses barely any lye, and cleanup isn't as much of a hassle. This also means minimal mistakes in the soap-making process.

Keep in mind that rebatched soap will not always have the most pleasant look when finished. To successfully rebatch your soap follow these six steps listed below:

You Will Need:

- Tools for melting
- Utensils
- The soap you want to rebatch
- Cutting tools like a food processor, a grater, or knife to cut your soap
- Bowls and containers for ingredients
- Measuring spoons/cups and a scale depending on what you add-in
- Molds

Step One:

Gather all equipment that will be needed, such as tools and safety equipment.

Step Two:

Cut or grate your failed or old soap batch into smaller pieces, or head to your local DIY store to purchase some clear glycerin. This is a great way to keep things all-natural

Step Three:

Melt your soap using either a double-boiler or microwave. The microwave will work wonders if you are a novice soap maker.

Microwave Heating:

- In a microwave-safe bowl, add your soap shavings and cover the bowl with plastic wrap.
- For 15-30 seconds, heat your soap shavings; if this has melted your shavings completely, then consider using shorter lengths of time. If your shavings have not melted, you can always leave them in for longer lengths of time.
- Keep checking and stirring your mixture after each period in the microwave. If the solution is not translucent, put it back in.
- Once the mixture is translucent, you can remove it from the microwave, being careful not to burn your hands, so oven mitts are advised.
- Start stirring the mixture gently.
- You can now add in any extras like dried flowers or roots.
- Make sure that your mixture has been evenly distributed before you pour the mixture into your mold. If you haven't added any extras, you can go straight to pouring.
- Let the soap cure and harden for the next five-seven days. You can ensure this by feeling that it's not soft when removing the soap from the mold.

Double Boiler Heater:

- You will first need to create a double boiler heater using either a stainless-steel or glass bowl placed just over the top, making sure the bottom of the bowl doesn't come into contact with the base of the pot.
- Place your soap or soap pieces into the bowl on top of the boiler.

- For every 1 lb/454 g of soap cuttings, you will need to add 4 oz/113 g of distilled water into the boiling pot.
- As the soap begins to melt, this is the ideal time to add any extras you might want in your soap.
- You must constantly stir when the water is boiling to melt the wax properly.
- It's a good option to record your results and process.
- Once your mixture is clear without any lumps, you can remove the mixture from the double boiler; set it aside to cool down.

Step Four:

Now that the soap is cool enough to handle, you can begin adding any extras you might like. These can include: dried herbs, rose petals, flowers, etc. You might also be tempted to add essential oils at the point; you can just make sure the mixture is well combined.

Step Five:

It's now time to pour the mixture into your desired mold and let it sit for five-seven days. It's important to keep the mold in a dry, safe place to ensure no spillage or potential contamination.

Step Six:

Make sure to record your results and the amounts of ingredients you use, as this can become crucial information during your next soap-making journey.

Simple Soap Recipe for Pure Glycerin

Ingredients:

- 283 g/10 oz Water
- 28 g/1 oz Your Choice Of Essential Oils
- 283 g/10 oz Coconut Oil
- 227 g/8 oz Castor Oil
- 227 g/8 oz Olive Oil
- 198 g/7 oz Sweetened Almond Oil
- 340 g/12 oz 70% Proof Alcohol Like Vodka
- 170 g/6 oz Vegetable Glycerin

- 1 Cup/128 g/4.5 oz Water
- ½ Cup/64 g/2.25 oz Sugar

Step One:

With your crock-pot set to a low temperature, you can slowly combine your oils, keeping an eye on the temperature.

Step Two:

In a fairly well-ventilated area, add your lye to your water to give it time to cool for the next 15-20 minutes.

Step Three:

Using your stick blender as a spoon, gently pour your lye solution down the shaft of your blender. Blend until the mixture reaches a light trace.

Step Four:

Cover and let set to reach the gel phase.

Step Five:

Once your soap has reached the gel phase, add in your 70% proof alcohol and glycerin mixing thoroughly. It might seem a bit thick or chunky at this stage, but as you proceed to blend your mixture, it will eventually smooth out.

Step Six:

Let your mixture sit for at least two hours.

Step Seven:

Once the two hours are up, you can now use your microwave or stovetop to heat the water and sugar. Make sure the sugar has been dissolved properly; set aside for later if the sugar has been dissolved.

Step Eight:

Once the two-hour mark has passed, you can begin mixing in your sugar-water solution, stirring to remove any air pockets within the mixture whilst your soap batter is still hot enough.

Step Nine:

Scoop away any foam that has risen to the surface.

Step Ten:

Add in your essential oils. (Optional)

Step Eleven:

Pour your batter into a mold, tapping the sides gently to remove any air pockets within.

Step Twelve:

Remove your soap from the mold when the soap has set to the correct hardness. The hardening process can take anywhere from two to three days, so it's advised that you have patience and not rush, as this can lead to your soap being damaged or unusable.

Four Natural Colourants

Below is a list of four natural colorants that you can use to naturally dye your soap without the use of mica powders, oxides, and pigments. (Keep in mind that these are not all the natural colorants that can be used)

Pink:

Ingredient	Colour or shade produced	Infused notes
Sorrel Root	Warm Pink / Salmon Pink	The root can be infused in soap making oils
Powdered Hibiscus Flowers	Soft Pink	Dried flower powder can be added into melt and pour soap
Madder Root Powder	Shades of Pinks / Red Orange	It can be infused in liquid oils
Cochineal	Dusty Pink / Purple Red	It can be used in cold soap process recipes as well as in oil infusions or raw.

Ingredient	Colour or shade produced	Infused notes
Rose Pink Clay	Pink / Red Brick	2.84-8.4 g/0.08-0.3 oz can be premixed in 5.69 g/0.6 oz of water before adding to your lye solution
Lady's Bedstraw Root	Coral pink	Infuse root into liquid oils
Red Palm Oil	Pinks / Orangey Reds	Add to liquid oils

Blue:

Ingredient	Colour or Shade Produced	Infused Notes
Activated Charcoal	Light Denim Blue	Add at 5.69 g/0.6 oz per 1 lb/454 g of oil
Blue Chamomile oil (Extracted from German Chamomile)	Blue	Use one-two drops of oil at trace or as desired
Indigo	Dark Blue and Green/ Light Blue and Green	Can be added at trace to the lye solution as well as with an infused oil
Cambrian Blue Clay	Shades of Light Greens / Blues	Add 5.69 g-8.4 g/0.19 oz-0.3 oz per 1 lb/454 g of oil. Before adding to lye solution, at trace, first mix in 5.69g/0.6oz of water
Woad	Green Blue / Grey Blue	You can add the powder to a small amount of oil or lye solution at trace. Additionally, it can also be infused in oil.

Yellow:

Ingredient	Colour or Shade Produced	Infused Notes
Curry Powder	Deep Yellow	Add 1.42 g/0.04 oz-5.69 g/0.19 oz per 454 g/1 lb of oil at trace
Saffron	Yellow	Infuse into oils before soap making
Lemon Zest	Yellow	Add finely grated zest either fresh or dry after trace
Yarrow	Muted Yellow	You can use dried Yarrow leaves and flowers to infuse oils as well as add yarrow powder directly to the soap at trace.
Rudbeckia petals	Yellow	Infuse petals into the lye solution.
Daffodil Flowers	Pastel Yellow	Use as a water or oil infusion or as a puree added to the soap at trace.
Safflower	Yellow / Orange Yellow	Add the safflower powder at light trace
Carrots	Yellow / Yellow Orange	Add puree into lye solution at 5.69 g/0.19 oz per 454 g/1 lb of soap.
Goldenrod	Pale to Mustard Yellow	Infuse fresh flowers into the lye solution.
Turmeric	Light Pink-Yellow / Burnt Orange	Can be infused in oils; discard spice afterward.

Black:

Ingredient	Colour or Shade Produced	Infused Notes
Black Brazilian Clay	Grey / Black	For darker shades, add 5.69 g/0.19 oz per 454 g/1 lb of oils.
Poppy Seeds	Blue Grey / Black specs	Premix with a small amount of oil before adding into lye solution at trace
Coffee Grounds	Black Speckles	Add used or fresh grounds at trace
Dead Sea Mud	Grey	Mix with a small amount of oil before adding to trace.
Activated Charcoal	Deep Black	Add to liquid oils at light trace; you will have to use more to get darker shades.

Clay Face Mask

Supplies:

- 1½ tsp/ 0.25 oz French green clay
- 1½ tbsp/ 0.75 oz aloe vera gel
- 1 tbsp/ 0.5 oz rose water
- Two drops of essential oil or an acne-reducing oil (Optional)
- 1½ tsp/ 0.25 oz Kaolin clay

Equipment:

- Bowl
- Spoon for mixing

How to Make a Clay Face Mask

1. Combine the green and kaolin clay into a container/bowl.

2. Add the aloe vera gel, essential oils of your choosing, and rose water mix and combine thoroughly till all the ingredients are fully incorporated.
3. The Face mask is ready to use. Apply the mixture to your face and let it sit for five-ten minutes; rinse off thoroughly. (Finish)

Sensual Massage Oil

Supplies:

- 18 tsp/ 3 oz Argan oil
- 12 tsp/ 2 oz Moringa seed oil
- 30 drops of an essential massage oil blend
- 2 oz. fractionated Coconut oil
- 18 tsp/ 3 oz. Jojoba oil

Equipment:

- Spoon for mixing
- Container/bowl
- Empty bottle small, medium or large

How to Make a Massage Oil

1. Use a spoon to mix together the jojoba oil, argan oil, fractionated coconut oil, and moringa seed oil in a small container. Make sure that it has been combined properly before starting the next stage.
2. Add the essential massage oil to the blend and adjust the amount of oil depending on your scent preference. Carefully pour the massage oil into a bottle or container and store it in a cool, dark space.
3. Once you're ready to use the essential massage oil, pour a small amount onto your hand and rub it into your skin. (Finish)

Chapter 10: Incorporating Hygge on a Budget

Hygging on a Budget

When it comes to Hygge and Hygging on a budget, it's essential to keep in mind that there are many activities that you can partake in at home that will cost you next to nothing, and most of these don't require you to go out and spend any money. Some such activities include:

- Wearing comfortable clothing
- Using essential oils (Optional)
- Eating a wholesome meal
- Listening to music

You can do these activities in the safety and comfort of your home with friends and family loved ones, or maybe you're just taking a day off for yourself; that's totally acceptable. There are, however, more activities that you can do at home. Keep in mind the aspects of Hygge when trying to incorporate Hygge into your activities.

To put it simply, when trying to incorporate Hygge on a budget, think of an activity that will help you feel relaxed that can be done in the comfort of your home without the need to spend money. However, spending money is acceptable, in reasonable spending amounts, though don't get carried away and spend it all in one go.

Prioritize Your Needs

When you go out shopping for your weekly/monthly groceries, you might get sidetracked and end up purchasing items that you may not need. So before you head out for the day, it might be wise to make a list of the groceries and household equipment you might need. Doing so will ensure that your needs are met and that the essential items are bought.

When prioritizing your needs, it's often that one forgets to prioritize "yourself." Therefore, take a couple of minutes out of your day to relax. There is no harm in doing so. Who knows, you may discover what matters to you. It's easy to get swept up in social media and online content in today's day and age. Most individuals strive to achieve what everyone else is looking for without ever really looking at themselves.

These pursuits could look like a new outfit, phone, or a set of abs; these things are all great if they matter to you. However, if they do not, just because it matters to someone else doesn't mean you need to add it to your priorities list.

Purchase Second-hand

In order to save money and have a little extra for luxuries, you might want to purchase second-hand as this is a great way to save on cash, and it benefits the environment too. This is not only a fantastic way to save money, but it's a clever way too.

You may be surprised as to what you can pick up in a second-hand goods store, so keep your eyes peeled for ads, flyers, and posters advertising second-hand goods for sale. Don't be shy when it comes to buying from a second-hand goods store; always barter the price down as most second-hand goods stores are willing to drop the price to make sales.

Hunt for Discounts

When looking for discounts, it's important to remember that spending money has been proven to make us feel guilty. However, this doesn't stop you from looking for bargains as this can, in some cases, make you feel less guilty.

There are a few methods in which to look for discounts, such as targeting your favorite store at a specific time of the year, visiting the shop's website (If they have one), or even signing up for their newsletter.

Additionally, we often have our friends and family tell us about deals they have found and vice versa, so don't be scared to look into the discounts further. This, in turn, generates a stronger bond between your friends, family, and loved ones.

As such, deal hunting is not just a way to enhance your social experiences and close relationships but also mitigate guilt.

Develop a Fund for Hygge

Suppose you'd like to create a Hygge area in your home of life but can't afford it at the moment; you can always save up. Open up a bank account specifically to make your life more Hygge; you may need to do a little research based on what you envision.

Start With One Place to Hygge and Then Move On

Sometimes it's essential to start small; this is especially true when making Hygge changes to your life. To make this Hygge dream a reality, start with one section of your home/apartment. You might just want to make your room a little cozier, like your bedroom or perhaps your dining area, so pick one priority area to start with before moving on to the next.

Conclusion

To conclude, even though you can achieve Hygge through the different processes that were discussed previously in this book, the term Hygge is more about acknowledging a feeling or moment. Although Hygge is a feeling, you can also incorporate it into other aspects of your life. By now, you should know more or less what Hygge entails and how to achieve it. So don't hesitate, start your Hyggelig lifestyle today.

Tak Fordi Du Læste Med (Thanks for reading)

Made in the USA
Middletown, DE
04 August 2022